NAVIGATING GRIEF AND LOSS

25 Buddhist Practices to Keep Your
Heart Open to Yourself and Others

KIMBERLY BROWN

Prometheus Books

Essex, Connecticut

 Prometheus Books

An imprint of Globe Pequot, the trade division of
The Rowman & Littlefield Publishing Group, Inc.
4501 Forbes Blvd., Ste. 200
Lanham, MD 20706
www.rowman.com

Distributed by NATIONAL BOOK NETWORK

British Library Cataloguing in Publication Information available

Library of Congress Cataloging-in-Publication Data Available

ISBN 978-1-63388-819-7 (pbk. : alk. paper) | ISBN 978-1-63388-820-3 (ebook)

♾™ The paper used in this publication meets the minimum requirements of American National Standard for Information Sciences—Permanence of Paper for Printed Library Materials, ANSI/ NISO Z39.48-1992.

For Denise

We don't know how we will grieve until we grieve.
—CHIMAMANDA ADICHIE[1]

I have come to see that the great matter of birth and death is not great because it's overwhelming and uncontrollable but because it is profound in its immense capacity to arouse a loving nature in us, bring attentiveness to living, and most importantly to seal an interrelationship between all that is born and will die. When we hear of a death we are reminded, like nothing else in life, that we are interdependent upon one another.
—ZENJU EARTHLYN MANUEL[2]

Contents

CONTENTS

FOREWORD

I'VE KNOWN KIMBERLY BROWN FOR MORE THAN TEN YEARS AND truly admire her good heart and her dedication to helping others, all of it underpinned by her practice of Buddha's wise advice.

We all want to be happy and don't want suffering; our problem is that we allow ourselves to be pulled from pillar to post, struggling to deal with what life brings us, especially loss and grief.

Buddha's genius is his deep understanding of the mind, the inner workings of our own cognitive process. He gives us the skills to become intimately familiar with our thoughts and emotions and to radically reconfigure them, thus enabling us to live our lives with courage and compassion, for our own sake and the sake of others.

Kimberly's beautiful book is full of such advice, not just for Buddhists, but for everyone.

—Robina Courtin, Buddhist teacher and editor

Preface

In August 2011, a doctor at a hospital in mid-central Wisconsin called to tell me my mother was in the intensive care unit. She explained that Mom was suffering from dehydration and kidney failure and had been brought by ambulance to the emergency room. Sitting on my couch in my apartment in downtown Manhattan, I was angry and impatient, interrupting the doctor to ask, "Is she dying?" There was a pause as she considered her words. "Well, I can't be sure . . . but it looks pretty bad. I think you might want to come here."

Which was exactly what I *didn't* want to do. My mom, suffering from chronic obstructive pulmonary disease as well as emphysema, had been in the hospital four times during the past year, discharging herself as soon as possible and refusing to comply with the doctors' instructions to eat, take her medication, and quit drinking and smoking. I thought this time would be the same as the others, and I was mad even as I booked a flight to Mosinee Regional Airport and began packing. My friend Stephanie came by to help me, and as I sorted through my drawers and closets, she said, "I think you should pack a dress." Annoyed, I asked, "What for?" To which she replied, "Just in case there's a funeral."

I wore that dress a week later. Despite knowing that she'd been in decline for several years, that her illnesses were progressive and worsening, that she was more than eighty years old, and that she badly abused her body, I was the last person to comprehend that my mother was dying and was utterly shocked when it happened.

When someone is alive, especially someone we love or know well, it's almost impossible to imagine that they'll no longer be here. Even if, like my mom, they've been sick for months or years, the irrevocable and mysterious nature of death feels almost beyond our comprehension. As a meditation teacher, one of the reasons I wrote this book is to remind myself—and you and everyone we know—that death and loss are normal, common experiences, and we can develop skills to anticipate and accept them, even when they're painful and sad.

Recently, the losses felt by my students, friends, family, and the world have been staggering. No one is immune to the effects of the coronavirus pandemic, and it's commonplace to get laid off from a job, end a relationship, cancel an important event like a wedding or graduation, lose a loved one to this terrible virus, or simply grieve the end of our ordinary interactions with our communities. That's another reason I wrote this book—to support all of us through grief and mourning, to remind us that bereavement is normal, and to let you know that you can go through it without being destroyed.

Buddhist students like me are continually reminded to recognize the impermanence of all things and to remember that every human will get sick, grow older, die, and lose all we hold dear. We're trained like this so we can face the truth of our precious and brief lives and help alleviate suffering for ourselves and others. Death and grief are unavoidable, but it's possible to learn to respond to this fact of life in ways that are supportive and strengthen our relationships. The practices and meditations in this book can guide you through divorce, layoff, unexpected change, even death—without becoming overwhelmed and shutdown, angry and blaming, or frightened and looking for a way out. Instead, these traditional contemplations, which are rooted in Buddhist teachings, will help you develop compassion and wisdom to experience your grief directly, with kindness, and to heal. They're designed to help you to experience all of your feelings, even the most painful.

No matter who you are or what your background—your race, sex, gender, ethnicity, culture, sexual orientation, class, religion, ability, or age—you will experience the vicissitudes of life and death. This fact forces *all* of us to confront our deepest vulnerabilities—that our most important plans can be ruined in an instant, that everything is impermanent and ever changing, and that our lives are transitory, fragile, and dependent on others. Some believe that this moment in time is the most dangerous and divisive of any in our human history, as we experience the devasting results of environmental damage and pollution, recognize the deep inequalities among us as a result of ignorance and greed, and face a mental health crisis rooted in a lack of compassion and a failure to prioritize the development of mindfulness and generosity. But perhaps it's also true that at no other time has it been so clear that we need each other like never before, that we are connected through our shared suffering and joy, and that we can use these terrible challenges to come together and share our abundant resources, reconnect to our wisdom and courage, expand our circle of care, and create a healthy and equitable world for everyone.

If you're reading this book, it's likely you or someone you love has experienced a loss, and neither I nor anyone else can tell you how to act or be. You might want to forget the events of the last few years, but I hope you'll use this book as a guide to bring you closer to both your sorrows and your gladness, so you can welcome life as it unfolds with presence, balance, and peace. It's intended to give you the confidence to reconnect to yourself and rediscover that you have everything you need to navigate grief and mourning. Its tools will help you welcome all that's in your heart—the painful, the delightful, the ugly, the beautiful—so you can become what you already are: a dear and loving friend to yourself.

Acknowledgments

Many people supported me in the creation of this book. My sincere thanks to Alice Peck, for her impeccable copyediting and guidance, to my agent, Steven Harris, for his confidence and encouragement, and to Jonathan Kurtz and the rest of the staff at Prometheus Books.

I thank my family and dear ones who've enriched my life and have been with me through its many joys and sorrows: Michael Davey, Lori Piechocki, and Madeleine Piechocki-Cannet.

I acknowledge the generosity and wisdom of my teachers, especially Sharon Salzberg and Venerable Robina Courtin, and so many others who've guided me on this path.

Finally, this book is based on my understanding of the Buddhist teachings. I trust readers will recognize the intention of the book and the spirit in which it is offered and overlook any misinterpretations or inconsistencies due to my ignorance.

Notes on the Practices

THE PRACTICES IN THIS BOOK ARE ADAPTATIONS OF TRADITIONAL meditations that I've learned through my Buddhist training. Their purpose is to help you comfort yourself, develop insight into your habits and behavior, and ultimately free yourself from suffering.

All the practices can be adapted for anyone of any ability. If you can't walk, sit. If you can't sit, lay down. If you have asthma or breathing difficulties, use sound instead of breath to anchor you. There is no wrong way to meditate as long as you're present-centered, paying attention, and meeting yourself with kindness.

Though everything in this book is a suggestion, not a requirement, I strongly encourage you not to skip the practices. In my experience, meditation and spending silent time alone with yourself is healing, calming, and reassuring—but only if you do it. It might be hard at first—you might be fidgety or bored—and that's okay. It takes time to get accustomed to paying attention to yourself in a new way. Don't give up—I'm confident you can do it because it was hard for me at first too, and with time and practice I'm comfortable and at ease with meditation, even on days when my mind is frustrated, dull, or filled with fast-moving thoughts.

Most importantly, be sure to use your wisdom while you're practicing. If you feel less steady and more overwhelmed, stop and try again later. If you feel too tired to meditate, take a nap. And if you're discouraged and want to quit, remember the reason you're practicing—so you can learn to take care of yourself kindly and skillfully through a difficult time and beyond.

CHAPTER 1

There Is Nothing Wrong with You

Let everything happen to you: beauty and terror.
Just keep going. No feeling is final.
—RAINIER MARIA RILKE[1]

MY PARENTS DIDN'T LIKE ONE ANOTHER AND IT WAS RARE FOR THEM
to share a joke or show affection. That's why I thought my Aunt
Lucille and Uncle Eddie were so special, although now I know they
were simply an ordinary happily married couple. Lu was a housewife
who'd never had a job and stayed at home to raise her daughters and
take care of her husband. Her friends and neighbors knew that if they
went grocery shopping or out to lunch together during the week, Lu
needed to be back by five o'clock to greet Eddie when he came home
from his job, at which point she would open a bottle of beer for him,
pour herself a glass of wine, and they would sit in their family room
overlooking the backyard and tell one another about their day.

Eddie was first-generation Irish, six foot four, with crooked teeth,
Coke-bottle glasses, and a loud laugh who hated travel and spent his
free time and vacations tending his backyard. His hands were hard
and rough from his job as a steelworker at Otis, installing elevators on
high-rise construction sites, including the Sears Tower in downtown
Chicago. Lu and Eddie were married for nearly thirty years when he

had a terrible accident at work—a scaffold came loose and he plummeted many stories down an elevator shaft to his death.

Naturally, Lu was devastated. Her daughters were grown but the eldest—a nurse—moved back home to be with her for a year. When her daughter left for her own apartment, Lu was still grieving but growing steady and caring for herself, spending time with friends, and doing volunteer work with the elderly parishioners at St. John Vianney Church. Still, her family was frustrated with her, because Lu continued to become upset when she witnessed or heard about any kind of accidental death. If a car crash, a building collapse, or a fall from a balcony was broadcast on WGN, the local television and radio station, it would send her scurrying out of the room weeping. Finally, her father told her, impatiently but not unkindly, "It's time for you to get over it, Lu."

I thought of this recently when my neighbor Sanjiv told me he was having trouble "getting over" a recent job loss. He'd worked at a boutique Brooklyn branding agency for nearly a decade and was one of a core group of employees who'd chosen not to leave the agency after the firm nearly filed for bankruptcy a few years earlier. At the time, the owners promised equity as a reward for loyalty, but before that was made official, they sold their firm for a large sum to a multinational company where Sanjiv was deemed "redundant" and soon after fired. Six months later, he was still angry about the unfairness of his former bosses in breaking their word and at himself for trusting them and not getting the deal in writing. Even after he found a new—and better—situation, he couldn't stop thinking about it and was frustrated and impatient with himself.

Like Lu and Sanjiv, lots of us receive messages that we should "get over it" and get on with our lives. But the truth is, it's not possible to just get over a painful loss quickly. Everyone's grieving process is on a different schedule; trying to do otherwise makes our feelings seem inappropriate or suggests something is wrong with us. Our connections to someone or something don't end when they or it ends, so it takes time to process and understand what's happened before we can make new decisions and move forward. If you've experienced a death, divorce, or breakup, got fired or laid off, or your house was destroyed in a fire or hurricane, or you've suffered any other profound loss, of course you'll be affected by it. But whatever you are feeling—if you're crying, not crying, sad, angry, energized and unable to sleep, or exhausted and unable to get out of bed—is okay. Any and all of your emotions, moods, attitudes, and sensations are part of the mourning process—normal reactions to significant loss and change.

There are no shortcuts. You can try to ignore your sadness by distracting yourself with work or get rid of fear by starting arguments with friends. You can tell yourself and your family you're fine while you're managing anxiety with binge eating or drinking too much. But none of these actions improves how you feel.

A note about prolonged mourning . . . If years have passed since you experienced a loss and you continue to feel overwhelmed, unable to fully participate in work, social, or family life, and your grief is not fading, you may be experiencing prolonged mourning, a chronic and persistent sense of grief. This isn't unusual after a profound life-changing event, and working with a grief counselor or joining a support group can help you through it. Sometimes we need extra help and skilled resources to fully transition through our bereavement process.

Unsuccessful attempts to deny, bypass, or discharge pain create disappointment or frustration and increase our suffering. *Why do I still feel so angry? When am I going to stop being so tired?* These can also make our feelings even more powerful, insistent, and overwhelming, because they need to be heard and cared for by *you* before they can resolve.

In Buddhism, equanimity is the wisdom that supports us through our sorrows and joys. It's the poignant understanding that the nature of everything is impermanent and ever changing; it's the opposite of believing we're able to control it all. With equanimity, we don't have to cling to happy moments, wishing they won't end, because we know they will—and it's okay. Rather, we can delight in our successes and joyful circumstances, knowing they will inevitably change. And in the same way, we don't have to push away or get overwhelmed by sorrow and loss, because we know this will change too. With love and compassion, we understand that we don't have to "get over" anything—we trust and are confident that we have all we need to meet whatever arises, including painful feelings—knowing they will come and go and change too.

In the Buddhist tradition there is a teaching called the Eight Worldly Winds—examples of the vicissitudes of life that all humans will experience. They are gain and loss; praise and blame; fame and disrepute; and pleasure and pain. Most of us are conditioned to desire the former in each pair and avoid the latter, but these circumstances aren't always under our control. A truly balanced and happy mind can weather these winds without grasping after the positive states or getting overwhelmed by the negative. Cultivating equanimity enables us to develop an unwavering internal strength and confidence that we can trust to support us through all the worldly winds in our ceaselessly changing and unpredictable lives.

Practice 1: Stay

If you're new to meditation, it might feel uncomfortable at first. That's because most of us have been taught to be productive, make things happen, get things done but have little experience with simply allowing life to unfold as it is without doing anything. It's also because meeting our emotions can feel unpleasant, so you might immediately want to change them into something pleasant or move your attention away from them entirely.

In this practice, you'll place your attention on your breath and simply "stay" with yourself. This is how to develop equanimity—quietly noticing your body, heart, and mind without getting up, distracting yourself with the internet, television, or work, or daydreaming away into a fantasy world. You'll become familiar with all aspects of yourself and your experience—the pleasant, unpleasant, and dull—without trying to fix or change or ignore anything. The more you practice, the more impartial you'll become to what's arising, ultimately meeting every moment—the good, the bad, the beautiful, the ugly—with equal interest, care, and kindness.

To begin, find a quiet place where you can sit or lie down without being disturbed. Set a timer for ten minutes, then keep your phone and devices out of reach. Turn off any music or television, and don't talk. Get still. Stop moving around and keep your eyes half-closed, looking at the floor or the ceiling without letting your gaze wander here and there. Bring your attention to your chest and take five conscious breaths, perhaps inhaling a little deeper and exhaling a bit more fully.

Place your attention here, on your chest as it rises and falls with your breath. You don't have to make anything happen, and if you do notice that you're controlling your breath, do your best to let go and just rest on your natural inspiration and expiration. You might notice emotions like sadness or anger and, accompanying them, judgments in the form of comments or thoughts like "Not this again" or "I wish this would stop" or as an impulse to get up to make dinner, to check your email, or to do anything except stay. When this happens, you can place your hand on your heart and gently say to yourself, "Stay." You can repeat this as many times as needed, breathing in "Stay" and breathing out "Stay." Continue like this for the entire ten minutes, resisting the urge to get up, to do anything except *stay*.

When the timer sounds, resist the urge to jump up and abruptly start a new task. Take a moment to mindfully stop the alarm, inhale and exhale a few times, and take a big stretch. Be sure to thank yourself and appreciate your time and effort.

CHAPTER 2

Change after Loss

We think of change as having lost something. Actually, change brings a new opportunity every moment, so there are limitless possibilities.
—His Holiness the seventeenth Gyalwang Karmapa[1]

EVERY YEAR ON THANKSGIVING, ALEXIS'S FAMILY DROVE TO HER great-aunt Tess's house in Detroit from their home in suburban Chicago. She and her younger brother loved riding in the back seat, looking out the windows, and trying to make other drivers wave and laugh, while watching the suburban sprawl turn to quiet, flat, winter-gray farmland and back again. Then they stopped at the A&W just outside the city, where their dad ordered four draft root beers and their mom pretended to protest the dangers of drinking soda.

When they got to Aunt Tess's old craftsman house, entering through the side door and walking up the few steps into the dining room, Tess always called to them from the kitchen, "The turkey will never be ready on time!" Alexis's Aunt Callie rushed to greet them and the two sisters hurried into the kitchen while Alexis and her brother dumped their coats on the bed in the guest room and excitedly ran down to the basement to see the other kids.

The kids—first and second cousins, a few stepchildren, and usually a couple neighbors—ranged in age from five to seventeen.

There was a big entertainment center against one wall with an old television where Tess's late husband watched his beloved Bears football games despite merciless mocking by his Lions-loving neighbors. There was a DVD player and a box of decade-old movies, and on Thanksgiving they watched *Die Hard* and *Bad Boys* until one of the grownups came downstairs and told them to put on something less violent for the little kids or they couldn't watch at all. One year, Alexis's ten-year-old cousin Michael, fascinated with competitive eating contests in Japan, choked on a turkey leg while demonstrating how fast he could eat, turning bright red as the rest of the kids froze, unsure whether to call an adult, until he coughed and vomited, and they all backed away in disgust.

When Alexis was twelve, Tess died and the tradition changed. Her mom, Aunt Callie, and their uncles decided to host Thanksgiving at their homes, but fewer people wanted to participate, and it just wasn't the same without Tess. Alexis missed the big gathering and didn't understand why it was so hard to coordinate it. But as she grew older, she understood that her great-aunt's death changed the dynamic of the family structure entirely. The last of four siblings, Tess was the thread that linked them together with their past, and when she died, they no longer had a common bond. Alexis exchanged letters with a couple of her cousins until she went to college, and after that she lost touch with her mom's side of the family entirely.

> The bad news: nothing is going to turn out the way you planned. The good news: nothing is going to turn out the way you planned. Without change, sickness can't be healed, new habits formed, and solutions to big problems like disagreements among nations or global warming are impossible. Change is the nature of all life, and each change has many consequences, some beneficial, some neutral, and others harmful or upsetting. We can use mindfulness—skillfully

paying attention to the present moment, with kindness—to help us notice when we're tightly holding on to "the way things should be" so we can be more aware of the different possibilities and choices available to us.

An ending—of a life, a relationship, a job, anything—creates unexpected changes, both welcome and unwelcome, and those changes have a ripple effect. Alexis's family started celebrating the holiday with just the four of them at their house, which was a little bit lonely. But it was also nice for her father to relax at home instead of driving, and her mother was a much better cook than Aunt Tess. And without the obligation to visit their relatives, Alexis's family were free to do something different, so twice they went on a holiday for Thanksgiving—once to Disneyland and once to Busch Gardens—and skipped the big dinner entirely.

We often believe that *the way things are right now* is the way things will be in the future, or the way things *should* be in the future. Perhaps it's the way that's familiar to us, or the way we prefer, or the fact that we simply don't—or can't—allow ourselves to imagine other possibilities for our future. But change is inevitable and if we hold tightly to these ideas, we suffer because they prevent us from experiencing the many possibilities arising from change. As Alexis and her family discovered, all endings have unexpected and unpredictable losses and gains.

I learned this too after I was fired from a job, which led to a series of events I could not have foreseen and that ultimately altered the course of my life. While in college, I worked for several years as a waitress at R. J. Grunts, a restaurant in Chicago. I'd planned to work there part time until I graduated, then move to suburban Evanston and find a job in human resources, but one day the management changed. They decided to do more with less staff and laid off several long-time workers, including me. I was surprised and angry, and my apartment lease was up, too, and since I really couldn't afford the rent increase, I impetuously decided to give away most of my furniture and stored the rest of my belongings in my friend's garage. Feeling down and discouraged, I decided to use my unemployment benefits to stay at my family's cottage in Wisconsin, intending to return home in a few weeks to finish up my last year at DePaul University. The cottage was an old three-room fishing shack without phone service or an indoor shower, and I spent the next week alone, reading *Lonesome Dove*, walking to the pond to see the beaver dams, and swimming from the rickety wooden pier. By the time my childhood friends Mark and Shawn canoed across the bay to invite me to dinner, I was feeling relaxed and less upset about losing my job. That night, when I rowed our aluminum fishing boat across to their much grander Adirondack-style camp, I met their friend Richard, who was visiting from New York City, and we started a long-distance relationship. Six months later I moved east to be with him, and all the plans and beliefs I had about what I was going to do, where I was going to live, and who I was going to be abruptly changed—all as a result of getting fired. Although Richard and I dated for only a few months, I stayed in New York, and twenty-five years later, I still live here.

We can all look back on our lives and notice how endings and loss changed their course in both positive and negative ways. This knowledge reminds us that we can help ourselves navigate the pain and confusion of grief by noticing when old ideas, beliefs, stories, and plans obscure our ability to see possibility and opportunity. By paying attention with mindfulness and kindness, we can learn to lessen our attachment to *the way things should be* so we can recognize the opportunities available in *the way things are*.

I've heard the following story many times—from a Zen teacher, a Theravadin nun, and even in the movie, *Charlie Wilson's War*. It's always attributed to the Buddhist tradition, but I've recently learned that it's an ancient Chinese story that predates the Buddha. Whatever its origins, it's a skillful teaching about the unpredictable nature of life and how we can meet change with clarity and wisdom to keep ourselves grounded, steady, and kind, no matter the circumstances.

Here's the story: the owner of a small family farm was working in her fields when one day her horse ran away. Her neighbors came over to help find the horse but it was gone. "Bad luck," they told her.

"We'll see," she replied.

The next day the horse returned, followed by three wild horses. The neighbors said, "How wonderful!"

The farmer said, "We'll see."

Soon after, the farmer's son tried to ride one of the wild horses but was thrown and broke his leg. The doctor came and the neighbors said, "How awful."

The farmer said, "We'll see."

The next week, the local militia came to their village to recruit young men for the army. Because of his broken leg, the farmer's son was not conscripted. The neighbors rejoiced for the farmer, exclaiming how lucky she was that her boy wouldn't have to risk his life in battle.

"We'll see," said the farmer.

Practice 2: Mindfulness

In the original Buddhist texts, the word *sati* is most often translated as mindfulness. *Sati* in the Pali language originally meant to recollect or gather, so its use in meditation describes a practice of noticing what you're paying attention to and choosing to gather your mind and become aware of the present moment.

Mindfulness is a popular concept today because our attention is so scattered. We're pulled away from the present by our computers, phones, televisions, and work, as well as our ideas, preconceptions, and the stories in our heads. If you're grieving a death or mourning a loss, you might be caught in memories or wishing things were the way they used to be. But we can't make decisions or take actions in the past. We can only do so here in the present. Healing doesn't mean forgetting about what happened, but rather knowing what's happening now, so we can take care of ourselves and respond appropriately to opportunities and threats. Mindfulness meditation enables us to do just that—to notice everything that's happening internally and externally so we don't have to chase after memories, block fears, or ignore biases and opinions. We can choose to return to this moment and meet it—just as it is—with kindness.

1. Unless you have health problems that prevent you from sitting comfortably, find a seat where you can maintain an upright posture. This could be a kitchen or office chair or even the edge of your couch. Avoid leaning against a pillow or hunching forward, and make sure your feet are solidly flat on the floor (add a book or a thick folded towel beneath them if they're not). Take a moment to align your ears above your shoulders and your shoulders above your hips. Tip your chin down very slightly

until you notice it is parallel to your shoulders. Now, imagine you're gently pulling a string up from the top of your head until you're in a position of relaxed alertness.

2. Close your eyes.

3. Bring your attention to the sounds around you, the soles of your feet, the air on your skin, the weight of your body, your breath. You don't have to make anything happen—you don't have to listen, or breathe, or taste, or figure anything out, or fix anything right now. All you have to do is *be*. After a couple of minutes, gather your concentration and place it on the center of your chest, where you can feel your diaphragm rise with your inhale and fall with your exhale. Use your breath as your anchor as you continue to sit quietly in meditation, your body tranquil and awake.

4. You can think of your mind as a ship in a harbor, tethered to an anchor. Waves and wind might push it around, but the anchor keeps it from blowing out to sea. In the same way, when your attention wanders from your breath because you're thinking or planning or telling a story in your mind, that's okay. You can come back to your safe harbor by gently recollecting your attention and placing it again on your breath.

5. Continue for at least ten minutes. Before you open your eyes and conclude your practice, take a moment to appreciate your time and effort.

While you're meditating, you'll likely start to notice that your mind has a seemingly endless display of opinions, judgments, worries, ideas, even images. It's okay. No matter what arises or what you get caught up in—thoughts about dinner, memories of your mom, anxieties about paying your rent or mortgage—gently notice and choose to return again to the security of your anchor and your breath. If you close your eyes and feel panicky, overwhelmed, or exhausted, keep your eyes open. Gaze softly down at the floor.

It's because we are unaware of this constant unconscious and habitual mental chatter that it obscures our senses and clouds our judgments and decisions. When we recognize all this busyness and activity, learn to let go of it, and return to our breath again and again, we free ourselves from reactive patterns. We can see that not all our thoughts are facts and not all our judgments are truths, so instead of responding thoughtlessly out of habit, we can make conscious choices with so many more possibilities available to us.

Meditation is called a practice because it takes time to develop your concentration, attention, and kindness. If it feels hard or you get distracted often, it's okay, just keep gently noticing what's happening and returning your attention to your breath. You can do it. I suggest doing this mindfulness practice every morning when you wake up before you get dressed or have breakfast. Starting your day with a friendly heart and a steady mind is a healthy habit to cultivate.

CHAPTER 3

When You're Angry

Somebody tries to say, "I'm sorry, I'm so sorry." People say that to me. There's no language for it. Sorry doesn't do it. I think you should just hug people and mop their floor or something.
                                        —TONI MORRISON[1]

LOSS CAN OPEN OUR DEEPEST WOUNDS AND UNLEASH OUR GREAT-est anger. After Christian's divorce, he lashed out at nearly everyone. His marriage had been floundering for years but he still was shocked and confused when his wife asked him to leave the family home, and he started arguing with anyone over anything. At his new apartment building, he harangued his upstairs neighbor daily about her junk mail in the lobby and persistently disagreed with and refused every reasonable suggestion his business partner made about expanding their lawn care business.

He didn't really notice or even care how he was acting until one afternoon, waiting to check out at a crowded grocery store in Queens, he screamed at an employee in outrage and dumped his shopping basket on the floor after someone accidently cut the line in front of him. Everyone stared as he stormed out. When he got to his car, he was shaking with rage before he put his head on the steering wheel and began to cry, realizing how much he missed his kids, his home, and his wife.

I reacted similarly after my eighty-eight-year-old father had a car accident. When the state trooper called me from suburban Chicago, I loudly insisted that he immediately call the Illinois Department of Motor Vehicles and rescind my dad's driver's license, even though the trooper kept explaining that it wasn't the protocol, it was Sunday, and didn't I want to talk to my father about it first? Then, when my dad got to the emergency room, I told the doctor to perform a CT scan and when she explained that it wasn't necessary, I screamed for her to get a gerontologist to call me and hung up the phone and marched into my husband Mike's workroom with my grievances. As he sat at his desk, wearing magnifying glasses while delicately painting a miniature Napoleonic battle figure, I ranted that everyone involved in my father's care was incompetent or lazy or didn't care. He took off his glasses, looked at me curiously, and said, "Kim, you can't keep this up," which just made me madder and I left the room.

When you're so angry that you feel hostility—an urge to harm or hurt yourself or others—and are about to say or do something irrational, mean, or stupid—*stop*. Stop talking, stop moving, stop texting or typing. Just take one breath, then another, then another. Feel your feet on the floor or the air on your skin. Put your hand on your heart and say, "I see you, anger, and I'm not going to leave you."

I finally realized how enraged and out of control I was the next day. I was yelling into the phone at a floor nurse about my dad's inedible breakfast and that I still hadn't spoken to a gerontologist when I noticed our sweet part-Siamese rescue cat Carmen slinking out of the kitchen in fear. As she left the room, I put my cell phone on the kitchen counter and sat down on the cool wooden floor in the hallway with my back against the wall. I took a few deep breaths. I could feel my racing heart and my churning stomach and my impulse to get up and make another phone call to another doctor. But I knew Mike was right—I couldn't keep this up. This level of rage and upset was making me sick and causing me to make decisions and say things that weren't helping my dad or me. So I stayed there, feeling the floor and the earth beneath it, and I noticed that I was very tense—my shoulders were near my ears, my teeth were grinding, my thighs were clenched—so I let myself relax a little. That's when I realized how scared I was—that under all this outrage and bluster was a vulnerable child afraid to lose her dad. My chest was heavy, I could hardly breathe, and I felt so sad and powerless that it was hard for me to stay seated and not get up and start yelling at someone so I didn't have to feel this way anymore. As I stayed still and felt my body and my heart, my anger subsided and I grew calmer. I realized the poignant human truth—my dad was old and injured and perhaps unable to care for himself anymore, he would inevitably die, and I couldn't change any of it.

Anger is a sign telling us, "No. I don't want this to be happening." It can be a wise signal that something isn't right—we've been hurt or others are being harmed—and we need to put a stop to it. But it also can be a misdirected warning to try to protect ourselves against painful loss, shocking news, or terrible tragedy. When this happens, the energy of anger provides us with an illusion of power and control that is not only false, but that often results in causing greater pain to ourselves and others. Skillfully working with this type of anger means allowing ourselves to respond to it with kindness, patience, and inter-est. It means telling ourselves, "Yes, this is happening," and requires that we slow down and pay attention to what's going on inside instead of reacting thoughtlessly to people and external circumstances.

Christian, in so much pain from the ending of his marriage and feeling abandoned by his family, only knew how to deal with it through anger. With anger, he could hide his hurt by blaming and hurting others, which helped him avoid feeling the sadness and grief that made him feel weak and ashamed. When he finally was able to sit down and quietly bring attention to himself, he felt all the feelings he didn't want to feel and cried. And although he was sadder than ever, he was also less angry and more at peace. As he learned to befriend his wounded heart, he began to heal. He could recognize his contribution to the failure of his marriage, extend patience toward his kids' upset and worries, and feel compassion for his wife's experience as well as his own. He had more resilience—and paradoxically more power—to help himself move through his loss, learn from his mistakes, and be more open to new possibilities for his future.

Having anger is not in itself a problem—it's how we react and relate to our anger that causes trouble. Like any of our emotions, we don't choose to feel anger—it arises unconsciously, so it's not effective or honest to blame or shame ourselves about it, and we don't need to get rid of it or cure it or try to hide it. All we need to do to effectively work with anger is to learn to identify it, stay with it, feel it in our body, and offer it kindness and gentleness. This creates the space and time we need to pause and make choices about what we want to say or do, instead of reacting uncontrollably with harsh or critical words or harmful behaviors.

Most of us find it hard to sit with anger because it's physically uncomfortable. The following meditation enables you to look deeply at the sensations and thoughts that arise during these moments, relate to them with openness and ease, and offer love to yourself and other suffering beings.

As this chapter reveals, I'm no stranger to anger. As a young adult, I used it as a way to feel powerful and right, and I rarely felt ashamed of it. But as I got older, I discovered that when I was angry, I often made bad decisions, hurt other people, or couldn't be heard because I sounded irrational or unapproachable.

The Buddha recognized the dangers of unchecked anger and described it as one of the "defilements"—mind-states that obscure our ability to see reality, leading to speech and actions that cause more suffering for ourselves and each other. In the Buddhist tradition, the antidote for anger is patience—learning to sit with and tolerate the emotional and physical distress arising without trying to fix it, change it, or push it away. This type of patience and restraint prevents our minds from growing wild with harmful thoughts and stories and enables us to uncover what might lie beneath our anger—fear, hurt, disappointment—and meet it with love, openness, and clarity.

Practice 3: Hearing the Hurt

Generally, the last thing you want to do when you're very angry is to just stop—stop talking, stop reading the news, stop thinking about what your partner just said, stop moving around—and sit quietly with whatever is happening. That's because your body and mind are unsettled, adrenaline is surging and with it a fight-or-flight response, anxiety, shame, and/or restlessness. This meditation encourages you to befriend and soothe your body and offer love to your heart and mind. You might need to try it a few times before you're able to settle down, and that's okay.

1. Stop everything you're doing or saying and take a conscious breath. Inhale and exhale. Do it again. And again.

2. Acknowledge that you're experiencing anger. Put your hand on your heart and say to yourself, "Anger is arising in me."

3. Sit down, stand, or walk. Put your hands on your belly and feel your body move as you breathe. You can repeat to yourself, "Anger is arising in me."

4. Keep breathing and start to notice your body. Pay attention to places of tightness, tension, pain, distress. Breathe into the places that need it.

5. Notice your thoughts. They might be rapid fire—"You always do this," "I'm right," "I hate you," "You're ruining everything," "Why don't you ever listen to me"—but just allow yourself to notice what's happening. If you get caught in them, return to step 4.

6. Offer yourself *metta* (also called loving-kindness) meditation. Repeat these phrases to yourself, *May I be open to the way things are. May I be at peace.* If you get lost, begin again.

7. Offer *metta* to the person you're angry with. Say these phrases silently: *May I be open to the way things are with you. May you be at peace.* Remember, you can always go back to step 1 and start again.

8. Stop saying the phrases, and quietly feel the rise of your belly as you breathe. Take a minute to offer *metta* to all of us struggling and confused humans by saying silently, *May we—may everyone—be at peace.* Then be sure to appreciate your willingness to bring kindness to all aspects of yourself by saying thank you to yourself.

CHAPTER 4

When You Know It's Coming

Do not ruin today with mourning tomorrow.
—CATHERYNNE M. VALENTE[1]

After nine months of cancer treatment, although nearly bald and often tired, my friend Denise seemed to be doing well. A quantitative analyst, she continued working full time, although instead of taking the El train to her office in Chicago's Loop, she took an Uber or worked from home. She still enjoyed inviting friends for dinner or getting burritos delivered from the Handlebar restaurant around the corner. She looked forward to reading Zadie Smith's new book, and she started watching *The Affair* on HBO. There were days when she had pain but it was well managed, and I, like many of her friends and family, believed that she was responding to treatment, that her cancer would go into remission, and that she would live a long time. We believed this despite the fact that we knew from the initial diagnosis that her type of cancer was resistant to standard protocols—we just didn't want to face it or think about it.

That's why I was shocked when, in December, less than a year after the doctors discovered the mass in her ovary, they said the chemotherapy wasn't working and the cancer had spread to her lymph nodes. The disease was terminal, although no one said it and I was afraid to even think it. Denise and I were more than friends—I loved her and she was part of my *mishpacha*—a Yiddish word that describes our closest family, related or not. With our friend Lori, we'd known each other for decades, traveled together, celebrated graduations and marriages together, and supported one another through divorce, illness, and parental old age and death. Not a day went by when the three of us weren't in touch via phone call or text. When Lori and I heard the awful news, she turned to me and said frantically, "Kim, if we don't find a treatment for her, she's going to die!"

Hearing and feeling Lori's desperation and grief, I felt it too—it was like being shot while wearing a bulletproof vest and I'd been knocked down and couldn't quite get up again. It was the first time either of us had expressed our deepest fear out loud. I took a long breath as I realized the reality of what she said and what I was about to say and I answered, "Yes. The odds are not good. I think she might die."

After I said that, I was filled with terror and dread. I didn't want it to be true and I did my best to manage it by trying to control and plan. I went home and researched and called universities and hospitals to schedule second opinions, learn about her suitability for experimental treatments, and explore alternative modalities for Denise. I downloaded a list of hundreds of clinical trials from the National Institutes of Health website, imported it into a spreadsheet, and began sorting through, trying to figure out what Denise might be eligible for and how we could get her into it. As I scrambled through the data, I could see that no amount of planning could assuage my foreboding and fear, so I closed my computer and rested against my old wooden library chair and closed my eyes.

If you're preparing for a loved one's end of life or another major loss and you're feeling depressed, rehearsing his death, and trying to predict or imagine the consequences of your life after he dies, you might be experiencing *anticipatory grief.* This is a type of grief that is similar to conventional grief but occurs before the loss. It can feel as intense as the actual loss and can prevent us from being present and kind to ourselves and others. If you notice you're facing this struggle, put your hand on your heart and take three deep and even breaths. Silently say, "I trust myself to meet whatever happens with kindness and wisdom." Repeat often.

I could feel my heart beating and noticed how tightly I gripped the armrest. Not only was I caught in fear, but I was also caught in hope. Although there's nothing wrong with skillful hope—using your wisdom to create and wish for positive outcomes—getting caught in hope means that you're demanding and grasping at a particular outcome. It's this type of hope that causes fear, and along with my desperation to find a cure for Denise to stop her from dying was an equally powerful fear of it happening.

Buddhist teachers often remind their students to let go of both hope and fear. That's because the two are deeply interconnected. Like two sides of the same coin, hope and fear are fantasies about the future that lead us away from the reality and wisdom of the present, causing us deep suffering and confusion. Although we can—and should—practice skillful hope—using our actions to benefit and not harm and ultimately to create conditions for a wise and compassionate future—how the future actually turns out isn't up to us. Instead of clinging to my need to find a cure, I could use my skillful hope and good sense to plan and prepare and let go of my demands or insistence that things turn out the way I wanted them to.

It was useful for me to explore drug trials for Denise, which quite possibly could benefit her health, but my insistence that she do what I wanted, that the researchers do what I wanted, and that the drug itself did what I wanted was impossible and was making me sick and afraid.

I thought about Rochelle, my neighbor who was a receptionist at a law firm in Brooklyn. Every time I met her in the hallway or saw her at the nearby coffee shop, she nervously told me she was afraid she was going to get fired and didn't know how she would find another job or take care of herself and her daughter. She confessed that her fear was upsetting her stomach so much that she'd stopped drinking caffeine. But when I saw her in the laundry room on Thanksgiving weekend, she told me, smiling, that she *did* get fired—and she was relieved. She already had another job lined up, which paid about the same, and she wouldn't have the long commute to Industry City anymore. She said, "I didn't have to be so scared, but I guess sometimes it's true that it's harder to look than to leap."

I knew that if I could look—and see how tightly I was clinging to hope for a cure for Denise's cancer—I could leap into this very moment and accept the unknowable future. I could still do my best to help her find an effective treatment and explore possibilities, but I could stop fearing the worst. Instead, I could be in the here and now, right this very moment, free from hope and fear. Because in this moment, Denise was alive, not dead. There would be plenty of time for mourning and sadness if and when she succumbed to her illness, but I didn't have to do it now.

The experience of dread—of something terrible about to happen that Rochelle and I felt—can be assuaged by bringing attention to the present and by having confidence in it. From that moment on, whenever I noticed my shallow breathing and roiling stomach, I offered kindness to Denise and to all of us who loved her. I reminded myself that whatever happened, I could trust myself to be with her through it and to treat her and myself with tenderness and clarity and that I would be okay, no matter how it turned out or how sad and heartbroken I might be.

Letting go of hope and fear means you can stop attaching your happiness and well-being to the future. Instead, you can be where you are today, with appreciation and kindness whatever the circumstances.

When you can relate to your life as it is right now, you're free from trying to control what you can't control and open to meeting life with wisdom and compassion as it unfolds.

Decades ago, before I formally studied Buddhism, I read *Zen Flesh, Zen Bones*, a compilation of koans—oral teachings—collected from the Indian, Chinese, and Japanese Zen Buddhist traditions. One of the most famous stories in the book—one that I've since heard told at many Buddhist centers—is called the "Tiger and the Strawberry." It describes the dilemma of a monk, chased off a cliff by tigers. He's hanging hundreds of feet above the ground, clinging to a skinny vine that will soon break. Tigers snarl at him from the edge of the precipice. The monk notices a ripe strawberry, plucks it, and puts it in his mouth and savors its sweetness.

That's the end of the story, and for such a long time I had only questions and frustrations about it. What does it mean? Why waste time eating a strawberry at such a precarious moment? Maybe the monk should toss it to distract the tiger? Maybe it's magic and the monk will be able to fly away? What should he do?

Only many years later did I understand why the monk savors the strawberry—it's because he is letting himself live without hope or fear and enjoying the present moment. Although the monk knows his death is imminent, as long as he stays in the present, he is free—to experience the strawberry and meet the next moment with openness and wisdom.

Practice 4: Facing the Present

Facing an impending death or possible loss can bring up tremendous hope, anxiety, and fear. You might feel overwhelmed and wonder what will happen to you when your loved one dies or if you lose your job. You might think you won't be able to bear the pain or take care of yourself. You may fall into catastrophic thinking, imagining the worst possible outcomes, like becoming immobile from grief or living on the street. We can use mindfulness to bring us back to reality, right here in the present moment, and to remember that we're okay and we will meet difficult situations when they arise and not before. This brief on-the-spot meditation can help you let go of terrible predictions about the future and support yourself with kindness and presence right now.

1. Notice that you're imagining the future, feeling dread, or worrying.

2. Stop. Stop. Stop talking, moving, thinking. Wherever you are, just stop. If you're at your desk, look away from your computer; if you're cooking dinner, shut off the stove and sit down at the table. (If you're driving, turn off the radio, breathe, and do the meditation later.)

3. Take a deep, full inhalation and say to yourself, "I am here." As you exhale, say to yourself, "I am now."

4. Repeat "I am here/I am now" in sync with your breath. Repeat this over and over as you sense your body—notice your feet on the ground and the air on your skin and any tightness in your belly, jaw, or shoulders. Keep breathing and continue repeating, "I am here/I am now."

You can continue for as long as you need, and you can do this practice as often as necessary.

CHAPTER 5

It's Not Fair: When a Young Person Dies

He came out of nothingness, took form, was loved, was always bound to return to nothingness. Only I did not think it would be so soon.

—GEORGE SAUNDERS[1]

I MET ASH AT A MEDITATION CENTER WHERE I WORKED. HE WAS twenty-seven years old, recovering from a traumatic brain injury from a car accident a few years earlier, and slowly regaining his ability to walk and speak clearly. The center, on the second floor of a nineteenth-century building on the Bowery in Manhattan, had no elevator, but despite his crutches, Ash managed to climb the steep, narrow steps to class every week and arrive at the door excited and happy to see friends and learn.

A few years later, after he'd swapped his crutches for a cane and was walking almost entirely on his own, he started having trouble recalling words. His speech was strange and garbled. Anticipating this was another side effect of his accident, he was shocked when doctors discovered a brain tumor unrelated to his traumatic brain injury. After surgery to remove it—which wasn't entirely successful—he was diagnosed with glioblastoma, a type of brain cancer that is very hard to cure. Tumors, even when removed, tend to grow back again and again, which was ultimately what happened to Ash. During the next few years, he had surgeries, radiation, and other therapies to slow the cancer's growth, until finally there were no more treatments available and he died.

Throughout his life, even at the end, Ash remained engaged with the world and with other people. He didn't become stoical or self-pitying, and although his illness was painful and debilitating, he met it with fortitude and laughter. The last time I saw him, he was at home, confined to bed, and had lost the ability to speak clearly, but he was alert and awake and could make himself understood. I explained that I wouldn't be back for a week because I was visiting my niece in Chicago for her high school graduation. Ash smiled at me delightedly, clapped his hands, and offered congratulations to her and our family. I felt so appreciative and grateful for his ability to be joyful and generous despite the circumstances. A few minutes later, his old friend Lara entered the room to visit, and once again his face glowed with excitement and joy and he grinned and waved.

> If you're a parent or grandparent dealing with the death of a child, I encourage you to seek additional support to guide you through this loss. Studies suggest that losing a child can cause the greatest and longest lasting stress a person can experience. Don't be afraid to use your personal resources—friends, family, community, clergy—and consider bereavement counseling as well as support groups. Two wonderful organizations, Griefnet and Hope for Bereaved, offer help for grieving parents and are listed in the resources at the back of this book.

Everything that happened to Ash seemed so unfair—his brain injury, the cancer, his death. He was so young, and it didn't seem right that he'd suffered so much, that he didn't get a chance to live a full life. People his age rarely face terminal illness or struggle with mobility and speech, and all of us—his family, friends, and peers—were shocked by what happened to him.

On the forty-ninth day after his death, all of us in his meditation community organized an event for his family and friends to remember him, say prayers, and meditate for him. The night before, as I thought about what I would say and offer to Ash, I remembered a teaching I'd heard a decade earlier at a Buddhist monastery in upstate New York. At a traditional Tibetan stupa and temple, built on a hill above the Hudson River, I sat with fifty or so others in a small shrine room. The space was dominated by a ten-foot-tall gold gilt buddha, photos of His Holiness the Dalai Lama, the Karmapa (the spiritual head of this particular Tibetan monastery), and the deceased former abbot of the center. I sat on a cushion on the floor with the other students. In the front of the room on a raised golden platform surrounded by prayer flags, *thangkas* (fabric painted with devotional images), an interpreter, and thousands of statues, icons, and drawings of bodhisattvas and buddhas, was an old Tibetan Rinpoche, or guru. It was almost 90 degrees outside and not much cooler inside, but he didn't seem tired or eager to conclude the lecture, which was already running long. I was hot, sweaty, weary, and ready to go; the next train to the city was leaving in thirty minutes and I hoped to get to the station in time.

The Rinpoche must have noticed that many of us felt hot, rushed, and distracted, because he encouraged us not to waste opportunities to practice and told us a story from when he was a teenage novice monk living at a monastery in Tibet many years before. One afternoon, a visitor brought news from his home village and informed the Rinpoche that his childhood friend had died—he'd accidentally drowned in the spring rainy season when he stumbled into a fast-running river. Rinpoche and this friend were the same age and had grown up together. He told us he couldn't believe it—the boy was so young and it was so unexpected—and he was very surprised and upset by the news. Later in the afternoon, when he saw his teacher, a much older monk, and told him about his old friend, his teacher gave him a look of annoyance and admonished him, "Why are you so shocked?"

Rinpoche explained to us that his teacher was not an uncompassionate man, but rather wanted him to notice his ignorance and remember his training and the truth of life—that everything is impermanent and death can happen at any moment, to anyone, at any age. I realized that I felt the same surprise and sense of unfairness about Ash's death as Rinpoche did about his friend's, and I shared the same ignorance and deep confusion about the nature of life as he once did. I still believed—despite overwhelming evidence to the contrary, despite my Buddhist training—that everyone is entitled to and can expect to live to old age.

Of course, it's true that getting cancer in your twenties, as Ash did, is unusual and unlikely. But it's not unfair that he died, although it was truly tragic and sad. The truth we all share is that no one of any age, anywhere, knows precisely when they will die or lose someone they love. For us to live fully with this unsettling truth requires that we acknowledge impermanence and change, be willing to mourn loss and face grief, and meet the unexpected with gentleness rather than denial or blame. The following practice will help you begin to cultivate this gentleness for yourself and others.

In the Buddha's time, people struggled to make sense of the loss of a child, just as we do today. When Kisa Gotami's infant son died, she refused to believe it. Cradling her dead baby, she ran from person to person, asking them to revive him, but everyone told her the baby was dead and she was crazy. Then she asked the Buddha to help her, and he agreed, telling her to collect a white mustard seed from every home in the neighborhood that had not experienced a death. Filled with hope, she went from house to house asking for mustard seeds, thinking that she could collect enough of them and that this would save her child. But in every household, someone had died. Finally, she realized, "This will be true for the whole town. The Buddha, who is friendly and sympathetic, saw this would be so."

Kisa Gotami later became a Buddhist nun, and we know of her from the *Therigatha*, a collection of teachings by the most experienced women practitioners of the Buddha's time. In it she explains that after her experience, she became free from suffering and the causes of suffering: "I've defeated the army of death, and live without defilements." Through her great loss, she realized the nature of impermanence and developed a steady mind and a compassionate heart. She learned to meet life without holding on to hatred or living in denial, but instead with a joyful heart, open to whatever might come.

Practice 5: You're Not Alone

The death of a young person is a particularly profound and painful heartbreak, and parents, family members, and even friends experience isolation and loneliness in their grief. You might feel that no one can understand what you're going through or can imagine your experience. But each year, more than eight million people younger than thirty die, leaving millions of families and loved ones sad and bereaved. This meditation encourages you to connect not only with your loved one and yourself, but also to include in your heart all the people in the world mourning a child, sibling, family member, or friend. The phrase you'll be using, "May we be happy and free," refers to the type of happiness that doesn't rely on external circumstances—a mind at peace and open—and to freedom from both physical and mental suffering.

1. Find a quiet spot where you can lie down comfortably. To begin, place your hands on your body—your heart or your belly—and notice how your body moves as you breathe. Take a few easy breaths, maybe inhaling a bit more deeply than usual, and exhaling a bit more fully. Notice how you feel and then breathe into any areas of tightness or tension that need a bit of kindness, patience, or love. Don't move on to the next step of the practice if you don't feel ready to do it—it's fine to practice with your body and breath for as long as you want.

2. Put your hand on your heart and make a connection with the young person that died. You might imagine his or her smile or a moment of happiness when you were together. Take a few breaths, and notice if you're feeling overwhelmed with anxiety, fear, or sadness. If so, stop and return to your breath. If not, you can silently offer this *metta* phrase to the person: *May you be*

happy and free. May you be happy and free. May you be happy and free. Continue silently repeating this phrase as though you're bestowing a blessing on your beloved. You can do this for just a minute or for as long as you like, while ensuring your breath remains regular and easy. Remember, you can always return to step 1 if you're struggling.

3. Let go of your connection with your loved one, and notice your body, your hands, and the feeling of your belly moving as you breathe. Pay attention to any places that are tight or tense, open or easy, cool or warm. Inhale, and as you exhale, send your kindness to any place in your body that needs it.

4. Now make a connection with yourself. You might imagine your reflection in the mirror, or how you looked at a time during your life when you felt peaceful, or simply let yourself feel *you.* Then give yourself the same *metta* phrase: *May I be happy and free. May I be happy and free. May I be happy and free.* Take your time, repeating these words as if you're giving yourself permission to heal and connect with your wisest self. Again, you can do this for as little as a minute or for as long as you like, being sure to pay attention to keeping your breath regular and easy and returning to step 1 if necessary.

5. Sustain this connection with yourself as you recognize all the people in the world who have also lost a young person. You might imagine someone on each continent or in specific cities, or just allow your heart to open to the many grieving people on the earth. Then silently repeat the same *metta* phrase for all of you: *May we be happy and free. May we be happy and free. May we be happy and free.* You can conclude the meditation by silently offering the great wish: *May all beings be happy and free from suffering.*

6. Before you get up, take a few deep conscious breaths and thank yourself for your care. Afterward, rest and give yourself whatever might make you feel nourished and comforted. Perhaps you have time for a nap, a walk, or a talk with a good friend. Pay loving attention to your feelings and remember you can always rely on your body and breath to anchor and ground you whenever you need.

CHAPTER 6

Sudden Death

"The earth will hold me," I would remind myself as I wrote between sentences, I was alive and I was a mother, and I could think and breathe and write, even as I felt the earth had been swept out from beneath me.

—ELIZABETH ALEXANDER[1]

WITH NO WAY TO PREPARE OR PLAN IT, A SUDDEN DEATH IS A TERRIble and devasting blow. Paige and her husband were in the mountains of Peru when they got a text that their daughter Sarah was in the hospital in Oakland with food poisoning. A day later, their son told them to come home immediately—she was in the ICU and wasn't expected to live much longer. Two days after that, she died and Paige felt her legs wobble and then give way as she collapsed to the hospital floor in exhaustion and grief.

Similarly, Kris and John were in shock when they learned that Tristan, their friend of more than three decades, had died on the Minneapolis METRO Green Line on his way to work. They'd known Tristan and his husband Casey since freshman year in college, and they helped Tristan care for Casey as he struggled with prostate cancer. When Casey died a few months earlier, they helped Tristan with the cremation and memorial and checked in with him often. He seemed to be doing well, but now, less than four months later, during his commute to the high school near Frogtown Park where he taught math, he had a heart attack on the light rail train, and emergency medical services was unable to revive him. After they got the phone call, Kris and John sat at their kitchen table, stunned and speechless.

When someone you love dies suddenly, you're faced with both shock and grief. You might feel physically and mentally stunned, unable to accept the reality of the loss. Paige felt such disbelief that she wondered if Sarah's death was a hoax, some kind of prank she'd played on them, and that she would soon reappear, laughing. Kris and John couldn't believe they'd never see Tristan again and could do little except lie on their bed and cry and hold each other.

> When you receive news of a sudden death, you might have an impulse to do something—to contact someone, to make arrangements, to figure something out. Or to scream at the top of your lungs and smash a few dishes just to ensure yourself that you're not dreaming. But don't. For a few moments, don't do anything, just stand there. Put your hand on your heart and take a few breaths and wait a few minutes before you speak or act.

When her dad died, Elizabeth thought it had to be a lie. She didn't grow up with her father and they weren't close, but after she had her son, he came to see them, and they stayed in touch. He'd always struggled with substance abuse and addiction, and when he moved to Reno, she stayed in Dallas, and their communication dwindled to a few holiday phone calls every year. But when Elizabeth's son was ten, Aunt Naomi came over to her house to tell her that her father had died a violent death. She sat at the kitchen table, an untouched cup of tea with honey in front of her, clutching an embroidered handkerchief in her hand as she told Elizabeth the story. Her dad had taken money from his girlfriend's retirement account and she pressed charges against him. When the police found him in a motel, he shot at them through the window. They stormed the room in riot gear and discovered him dead from a self-inflicted gunshot wound. Aunt Naomi sat quietly while Elizabeth's mind reeled. Her dad had never been violent in the past and he always said he hated firearms. The last time they'd spoken, he'd given no indication that he was struggling more than he usually was, and she wondered if she could have prevented the whole situation by asking him if he needed money. She started to ask her aunt, but Naomi stopped her and said, "I don't think we'll ever have the answers," and sadly, Elizabeth realized she was right.

When sudden tragedy strikes, it might feel like it's too much to bear or that it's totally unreal. We might wonder how we will get through it or make sense of it. But when it happens, it's important to remember that we don't *have* to get through it or make sense of it, at least not immediately. We need only let ourselves rest in the unfolding of life—we can just be here in reality with kindness and patience, the way things are right now.

If you've been at an art or history museum, you've likely seen paintings and statues of the Buddha, often depicted sitting in meditation with his left hand upright on his lap and his right hand touching the earth beside him. This gesture is the *bhumisparsa mudra*—the *earth witness seal* that the Buddha made at the time of his enlightenment. Legends tell us that he was challenged by his rival to explain who gave the Buddha the right to awaken, and the *bhumisparsa mudra* was his response. By touching the earth, the Buddha is saying that the earth gave him—and all of us—the right to see reality clearly and that touching the earth is evidence of seeing that reality clearly. Even—or especially—after a great loss, we can all reach out and touch the earth at any time for a reality check—to let ourselves know that we are here, we have every right to be here, and that we are alive and awake to what is happening right now in this moment, no matter how painful or confusing it might be.

Although a sudden death seems like a big surprise, we all know it's not; it's just that we tend to forget that our lives are impermanent and vulnerable and could end at any moment. One practice from the early Buddhist teachings is designed to help us remember: the Five Contemplations, or the Five Remembrances. It's a way to understand reality and prevent us from denying or rejecting the truth. If you recite the reminders every day, you might find yourself less surprised by the impermanence of life and more compassionate to yourself and others, because recognizing the brevity and fragility of our own lives means recognizing the poignancy and preciousness of *all* lives.

The Five Contemplations are:

1. I am of the nature to age and grow old. There is no way to escape aging and growing older.

2. I am of the nature to get sick. There is no way to escape sickness.

3. I am of the nature to die. There is no way to escape death.

4. All that is dear to me and everyone I love is of the nature to change. There is no way to escape being separated from them.

5. My actions are my only true belongings. I cannot escape the consequences of my actions. My actions are the ground upon which I stand.

Practice 6: Standing on the Earth

You don't have to take a formal meditation posture or a special seat to gather your attention and feel your feet on the earth. Try this exercise anytime you feel swept away by shock or confusion or when you feel unsteady and ungrounded.

1. Stop what you're doing and stand up. If you're unable to stand because of disability or health reasons, stay seated and adapt this practice to your ability.

2. Bring your full attention to your feet. Feel the soles, the toes, the tops of your feet. Notice the weight of your body and feel the ground beneath you.

3. Raise your arms above your head. Push down gently into your feet, straightening your knees. Notice you're securely attached to the earth even as you're stretching to the sky.

4. Let your arms hang loosely by your sides. Take a few breaths, inhaling to your toes and exhaling from your belly.

5. Repeat as necessary.

6. Before you get up, take a few deep conscious breaths and thank yourself for your care. Afterward, rest and give yourself whatever might make you feel nourished and comforted. Perhaps you have time for a nap, a walk, or a talk with a good friend. Pay loving attention to your feelings, and remember you can always rely on your body and breath to anchor and ground you whenever you need.

CHAPTER 7

If Your Family Disappoints You

"Who in the world cares for you? or who will be injured by what you do?"
Still indomitable was the reply—"I care for myself."
—CHARLOTTE BRONTE[1]

I WAS TWENTY-FOUR YEARS OLD, A COLLEGE SOPHOMORE LIVING with my boyfriend on the North Side of Chicago, commuting on the El train to school and my job at a popular Lincoln Park restaurant. I'd been a waitress there since before I enrolled at DePaul University and worked three or four shifts a week on weekends and after class to pay my share of rent and expenses. My boyfriend and I had known each other for a few years, and although our relationship felt serious and committed, the truth was we had little in common and resented each other for it. The cozy first-floor apartment with the backyard was our second attempt at living together, and it wasn't going very well. I was busy and frustrated that my boyfriend didn't contribute to household tasks like cleaning or laundry. He was annoyed that I wasn't home much. When I was unexpectedly and unfairly fired from my job by a new manager, it became clear that our relationship was unlikely to weather the additional financial strain and emotional stress.

I was feeling sad, stuck, and desperate. I looked through the *Reader* (a local weekly newspaper) searching for affordable apartments but didn't know what to do—how could I rent an apartment without a job or income? I didn't want to wait tables again but since I had no other work experience and believed I was unqualified to do anything else, why would anyone hire me? I was alone and lonely, regretting the breakup, missing my friends from the restaurant, and watching all the plans I'd made fall apart. My belly was tense and tight and I wanted someone to help me feel better. As I watched my boyfriend and his friends from his softball team pack up his drum kit, I sat on the front stoop, glowering at the beautiful irises I'd planted, and called my mom. When I blurted out what was happening and how upset I was, she interrupted me. "Kim, I hope you're not asking me for money because I don't have any to give you." I defensively explained that I only wanted her to listen before I angrily said goodbye, ended the call, and sobbed.

I was mad and felt abandoned. I wondered why I didn't have a loving, caring mother who I could count on when I needed her. As I grew older, I learned that I wasn't alone—in times of crisis, many families struggle. The stress it causes can compound problems that already exist or reveal long-held resentments and conflicts.

That's what happened with Jerry's family. He had been his elderly mom's primary caregiver for a decade, ensuring she went to the doctor, maintaining her yard, and shoveling the snow at her old Wisconsin farmhouse. He lived nearby, but both his sisters were in Minneapolis, a four-hour drive away. Jerry resented the responsibility and his sisters felt left out and worried that he was controlling their mother's decisions and finances. By the time she died, all of the siblings were angry at each other. Although the house was small, in disrepair, and contained little of real value, while they cleaned and prepared it for sale, the sisters and Jerry fought over every item—from a broken grandfather clock to a collection of cookie jars. Finally, after his sister denied a request that his wife be allowed to keep a pair of earrings because his mother had promised them to her, Jerry refused to attend the funeral.

It may seem like an extreme reaction, but Jerry's situation is not an unusual one. Contrary to so much of what we're taught to believe, not all of us have loving, caring families. Many people grew up in households with alcoholism and conflict, physical and emotional abuse, neglect or cruelty. Even if you were raised in a stable environment, you may have parents or siblings who just aren't reliable, interested, or able to offer support, guidance, or empathy. We've been told to expect that we can count on family members in times of distress or that families come together during difficulties, and when that doesn't happen, it can be hard to accept. It took me many years to understand that I couldn't lean on my mother and she couldn't support me when I was struggling because she was suffering too, just like Jerry and his family were.

The Buddha's first teaching tells us that suffering—sometimes translated as *dissatisfaction*—is a universal feature of the human experience. Everyone suffers, and families are no exception. The Buddha also teaches us that we can be free of our suffering—our dissatisfaction with the way things are. The way to freedom is by our understanding our suffering directly, by experiencing it with kind and patient attention. In this way, we can see its causes—the poisons of greed and neediness, hatred and aversion, ignorance and boredom—and take appropriate actions to stop creating these poisons. Unless we choose to do this, we'll continue to suffer. Appropriate actions to reduce our suffering include clear intentions, healthy decisions, and beneficial and nonharmful behaviors for yourself and others. My mother didn't know how to stop drinking or pay attention to her body's needs and never learned to care for herself, so she couldn't care for me, even (or especially) when I really needed her. Jerry's family couldn't recognize that the loss of their mom was exacerbating their old hurts and resentments, making it impossible to communicate and empathize.

We can't understand or alleviate our own suffering if we haven't developed, been taught, or been shown much compassion. Compassion—the ability to be with suffering without judgment or blame—is necessary to allow ourselves to directly experience our struggles and open our hearts to ourselves with empathy. It's a quality that enables us to be with the difficulties in life without ignoring, looking away, or becoming overwhelmed by them. Compassion acknowledges and holds suffering—our own and that of other people—with the gentleness of a dog carrying her puppy in her mouth. It enables us to be present for difficult feelings and terrible circumstances and to take whatever action we can to comfort ourselves and others.

> Don't confuse compassion with passivity or stupidity. Compassion doesn't mean giving everyone everything they want, and it's not codependence—I give you want you need and you give me what I need—either. In fact, compassionate people are able to say "I love you, *and* no" without feeling ashamed or guilty. Similarly, wisdom means knowing what you can control and what you can't. If you can alleviate the suffering of others or yourself, then do it, but if you can't, use compassion to support yourself or another person through a difficult situation without avoiding it or continuing to try to fix it. It's normal to have sorrows as well as joy, and sometimes acknowledging pain and hurt and sitting with it—refraining from giving advice, blaming, or controlling—is the best and only action we can take.

When members of a family like Jerry's are already in conflict, or like my mother, are deeply troubled, they're unable to support and care for us when death, divorce, or traumatic events occur. The stress and pain of the loss is too overwhelming. This is why people behave badly during times of crisis or need. We've all seen it—the super-close adult sisters who argue at the end of each vacation together, unable to admit their separation anxiety; the father who cancels or doesn't show up for his son's wedding, still too upset with his ex-wife to be in the same room with her. They're not behaving out of malice or indifference, but from the inability to offer self-compassion and kindness to their difficult feelings and painful states of mind.

Instead of insisting, demanding, or feeling frustrated when our family can't be there for us, we can use our wisdom to recognize that it's not our fault or in our power to make them act differently. Then we can reach out to reliable resources who *are* available—other family members, friends, therapists—who are able and want to listen, empathize, and support us. And we can use our compassion to recognize that our unreliable family members are suffering, just as we are, and to extend our compassion to include them. Perhaps Jerry could have asked his sisters to share what his mother's possessions meant to them and explained that he resented that, as the only brother, he was always expected to defer to their needs. Or I could have stopped denying that my mom was an alcoholic and unable to cope with her own feelings—not to mention mine—and called a good friend instead of her. Even if the people we love can't give us the attention, kindness, and compassion that we need, we can give it to ourselves.

When my dad was very sick and being difficult—resisting help and demanding his car keys—I burst into tears, feeling so discouraged and alone. I decided to sit down on the couch and be quiet by myself for a few hours. At first, my thoughts continued a one-sided argument with my dad. But I kept remembering to come back to what was happening right now—the cool air from the window, my upset stomach, and all the pain and tightness in my heart. I said to myself, "Kim, you're really struggling and it's okay," and when I did, I sighed and felt my body relax.

Meeting suffering and developing compassion is a paradox—the friendlier and more familiar we become with our pain and struggles, the less troubling they are to us. As I sat quietly with myself, I became less alone and less concerned about what my dad thought or did. I stopped avoiding my upset and anger and instead looked directly at it with kindness. I opened my heart to myself and felt the sadness of having an unreliable father who couldn't support me—but realized *I* could. When I opened my heart to myself with patience and awareness, I became what I needed and wished for—a loving and supportive presence.

The Five Spiritual Faculties, sometimes called the Five Strengths, are qualities that support the development of a steady mind and open heart. Found in all Buddhist traditions, they are:

1. Faith

2. Energy

3. Mindfulness

4. Concentration

5. Wisdom

I was surprised that faith is the foundational strength because I've always thought having faith meant blindly giving up your power to a god or religious dogma. But in the Buddhist tradition, faith is based not on what we believe or have been told—it's based on our direct experience. Faith happens when we recognize our internal resources—our compassion, wisdom, and kindness—and know that we can count on them for support. Faith also happens when we use tools of contemplation and meditation, and experience for ourselves that they work, enabling us to understand our minds and see reality clearly. When we have faith in ourselves and practices like *metta*, gratitude, or self-compassion, we are less doubtful and more confident that we contain all the resources we need to benefit ourselves and others.

Practice 7: You Support You

When you're looking *outside* of yourself—for someone to put a hand on your shoulder to ease your pain or to listen to your troubles—take a breath and turn your attention *inside*, remembering that you are here for you, and try this meditation.

1. Find a quiet place where you can sit or lie down without being interrupted. Turn off your devices—computer, television, music player. If you like, you can set a timer on your phone for fifteen minutes, then put it somewhere out of your reach and line of sight. Let yourself get still and don't move around.

2. Close your eyes and notice the weight of your body on the chair or the floor. Exhale and allow yourself to get heavier. Take a few deep inhalations, and as you exhale, continue to relax and rest into the support of the earth. Do this for a few minutes.

3. Notice if any difficult feelings, pain, or struggle arise and what your reaction is. Maybe you're feeling regretful and letting yourself ruminate, feeling sorrow and talking yourself out of it, or your throat is tight and you're ignoring it. Keep breathing and if you feel like getting up or if your mind is distracted or busy, know that it's okay. Give yourself permission to stay as you put your hand on your heart, taking a deep inhalation, and exhaling into the support of the earth.

4. After doing this for a few minutes, think of someone you know who is struggling right now—a friend or loved one, someone with whom you have an easy affectionate relationship, not your difficult boss or an unsupportive family member. You can imagine him or her sitting near you or just have a

sense of the person as you recite: *May you accept this moment as it is. May you be at peace.*

5. Take a few minutes to repeat these kind and wise words like you're offering a blessing to your friend. If you lose the connection or start thinking of something else, it's okay. Just come back to your breath, reconnect with your loved one, and start the phrases again. When you're ready, you can let go of this connection, take a few breaths, and notice whatever is arising.

6. Next, make a connection with yourself—imagining yourself as a child or feeling your presence. Now, give yourself these same wise and kind words: *May I accept this moment as it is. May I be at peace.*

7. Take your time and keep repeating these blessings to yourself, as if you're giving yourself a gift. Remember, if your mind wanders, it's okay. Return to your breath, reconnect, and begin again. Take your time, and after five minutes or so, release this connection to yourself, take a few breaths, and notice whatever is arising.

8. Finally, make a connection with your unsupportive family member or anyone who you find difficult or frustrating. You can imagine this person as you know them, or you might imagine them as a child. Or just let yourself sense their presence. This time, repeat the following phrases: *May I accept you as you are. May you be at peace.*

9. Continue to silently give this wisdom and compassion, knowing that, just like you, this person is suffering. If at any time you feel overwhelmed or upset, stop. Go back to offering the phrases to your friend or to yourself, and return to this unsupportive person when you can. It's called a "practice" because it takes time to build our capacity for compassion and develop our concentration.

When you conclude the meditation, take one minute to imagine all the humans in the world who are like us—suffering and confused. Give the world your compassion by repeating this phrase a few times: *May we accept ourselves as we are. May we accept each other as we are. May all beings be at peace.*

As always, be sure to thank yourself and appreciate your efforts to alleviate suffering and to bring compassion to yourself and others. Your intention is rare and valuable.

CHAPTER 8

Being Present at the Moment of Death

*I am who I am because somebody loved me, somebody cared for me,
and somebody attended to me.*

—CORNEL WEST[1]

I TOOK A TAXI FROM THE AIRPORT DIRECTLY TO ASPIRUS HOSPITAL
in Wausau, Wisconsin, where a receptionist directed me to my mom's
room in the intensive care unit. When I entered, she was asleep, an
oxygen tube in her nose, an IV in her arm, and she was hooked up to
several large, loud monitors in a tiny, cold room filled with equipment.
She looked weaker and thinner than she'd been when I saw her nine
months before. I rummaged in my tote bag for Carmex and smeared
it on her chapped lips, and her eyes fluttered open.

"Mom, how're you feeling?"

She rasped, "Terrible. My mouth is so dry . . . can I have something to drink?"

I picked up a plastic cup of water and navigated a straw to her
mouth as she tiredly leaned forward and sipped. "Thanks, that's
enough," she said, leaning back and closing her eyes. I settled into
my chair and put my hand on her arm, and she abruptly turned
toward me and said, "Wait a minute, who are you?" I told her and
she laughed, "Oh Kim, it's you! I thought you were the nurse. I really
can't see well anymore."

Later I sat in the waiting room with Dr. Patel, the physician on duty. He had no history with my mom and he made his indifference clear. "Your mom is an alcoholic. She's also been taking painkillers and Ativan, and when she was admitted she was severely dehydrated and confused. Her COPD has gotten worse and her kidneys are barely functioning." I asked if he thought she was dying. He stood, looked at his watch, and said, "Yes, I think you should be prepared for it." Then he shook my hand and left the room.

The next day, my friends Lori and Denise drove up from Chicago. They were there when Dr. Patel and a nurse talked with my mom about hospice care and she agreed to it. "Kimmy, the doctor told me I'm not gonna get any better. I don't want to live like this; it's terrible gasping for air. I really can't take it. I'm ready to go," she said weakly but with clarity. She noticed the look on my face and said, "Don't worry about me, honey. I'm not afraid to die. I'm not afraid to go to Jesus. I've had a good life. I can't take it anymore . . . it's too hard."

Lori started to cry and said, "I love you, Joyce," and my mom said, "I love you too, Lori. I love all you girls. I love you, Denise and Kimmy."

We all cried.

A few hours later they wheeled her in her bed to the hospice floor, a bright, spacious room with big windows overlooking a landscaped courtyard with trees and birds. Lori and Denise and I stayed there for the next few days, sleeping on large recliners. During the day we read and chatted with each other and talked to my mom, and in the evening, we went for dinner at the Red Eye Brewery.

No matter how much you plan for, expect, or prepare for it, being with a dying person is a physically and mentally unsettling experience. If you're feeling overcome or overwhelmed, take a deep inhalation and imagine you're breathing in your fear. When you exhale, imagine you are breathing out clear, bright, serene light. Do this for a few minutes as often as you feel you need to.

Many people die in the hospital like my mom, but an increasing number of Americans are dying at home with hospice care, so even more people are experiencing their loved ones' dying process directly and feeling unsure and afraid. When Hector's sister was dying of breast cancer, she was in her suburban condominium in Coral Gables, her tiny rescue Chihuahua El Rey by her side, along with three siblings, her ex-girlfriend, and several neighbors. Hector wanted to be there too, but he was so distressed by how she looked that he stood in the doorway, unable to sit by her side. After she died, he felt guilty about it for a long time.

Watching and waiting for someone to die can be as distressing as it is sad, especially if you don't know what to expect. The human body doesn't easily give up living, and dying is hard. Most of the time it's not peaceful and it's not at all like "just going to sleep." Many people, like my mom and Hector's sister, have labored and loud breathing; they moan and sigh loudly, their mouths open, cheeks sunken, skin gray; and they grasp the sheets and clench and unclench their hands. Their suffering is difficult to witness, and I felt lucky that Denise and Lori supported me. Together we did our best to stay calm and peaceful and reassure my mom, even though we were all afraid and wished we could do more for her.

I was also supported by a Buddhist practice that helped me to feel that my mom and I were surrounded by seen and unseen loving beings. "Calling the Lineage" is a traditional ritual to remember the kindness of your teachers, their teachers, their teachers' teachers, their teachers' teachers' teachers, and so on—all the way back to the historical Buddha. It's an expression of appreciation and a recognition that all we've learned came to us through the past kindnesses of others. In the same way, all of our lives are the result of past kindnesses that we've received from others.

When I felt shaky and afraid, I sat at my mom's bedside and breathed and called my lineage—all of the people and animals that had cared for me throughout my life. I imagined everyone who helped me since childhood—my parents didn't do such a great job, but my aunts showed up for me, and many kids at school, and my second-grade teacher who could see I was struggling at home and patiently let me hang out with her at her desk after school, and my sweet dog Marshmallow who was always happy to see me. I remembered my first boyfriend, Dori the waitress who gave me career advice, my favorite college professor, and my sweet cat Simone. I thought of the nurses who were taking such good care of my mom, and of course dear Lori and Denise there with me. As I did, I could feel all the love I'd received and was still receiving and grew stronger and more solid for it. I realized that being with a dying person may seem scary or strange, but it's actually the most natural thing in the world. It's a deep connection to our shared humanity and the brevity and poignancy of all our lives.

At a Zen center nearly two decades ago, I sat on the floor on a cushion and listened to a teacher read the great Buddhist master Thich Nhat Hanh's beautiful explanation of the interbeing of all life:

If you are a poet, you will see clearly that there is a cloud floating in this sheet of paper. Without a cloud, there will be no rain; without rain, the trees cannot grow; and without trees, we cannot make paper. The cloud is essential for the paper to exist. If the cloud is not here, the sheet of paper cannot be here either. So we can say that the cloud and the paper inter-are.[2]

At the time I thought these words were simplistic and maybe even trite, like saying "We're all one." But Thich Nhat Hanh doesn't mean we're all one. He means that we exist interdependently in a relational ecosystem we call earth. That all of us on the planet use, exchange, and ultimately become air, food, water, and sunlight. When we die, nothing of us disappears or vanishes—we continue in different forms within the ecosystem, which is why Thich Nhat Hanh is right—if you pay attention, you actually can see a cloud in a piece of paper.

Practice 8: A Lineage of Kindness

In the Buddhist tradition, all the different traditions honor their lineage by offering thanks to their current teachers, their teachers' teachers, their teachers' teachers' teachers, and so on—going all the way back to the historical Buddha. It's done as an expression of appreciation and a recognition that the teachings and practices supporting students in the present were created and passed down to students by many other people from the past. In the same way, each of us is the result of past kindnesses—an unbroken series of beneficial deeds and actions that we've been offered by countless other beings. And when we find ourselves in difficult situations, like a death or a divorce—we can recall our Lineage of Kindness—all these living beings that have helped and guided us, who have supported and taught us. We know we're not alone as we remember the love we received and are receiving in each moment.

1. Find a quiet place. Shut off your devices. Sit or lie down comfortably, stop talking, and get still. Take a few deep breaths and close your eyes. Bring your attention to the rise and fall of your chest as you inhale and exhale.

2. Place your hands on your heart and imagine the beginning of your Lineage of Kindness. Consider your grandparents' love for your mom or dad when they were children, or imagine a stranger offering a seat on the bus to your pregnant mom or the healthcare workers in the delivery room helping you when you were born.

3. Take a few deep breaths as you pay attention to your feet and the weight of your body. Recall or imagine the kindnesses you received throughout childhood. People who hugged you and helped you learn to walk. Strangers who smiled at you. Students

at school who told you jokes or shared their pen or their lunch with you. Family members[3]—your mom, dad, cousins, siblings, even pets—who comforted you when you cried, cooked meals for you, celebrated your birthday, cared for you when you were sick. Your date for prom, your partner in science class, the kid you cut school with, your best friend's sister who let you play basketball with the older kids.

4. Take some more deep breaths, paying attention to your feet and the weight of your body. Recall or imagine the kindnesses you received in your adult life up until today—the person who hired you for your first job, people you dated, vacations or trips with friends, the birth of your children, the pastor who married you, the lawyer who helped you through a divorce.

5. Continue taking deep breaths and paying attention to your feet and the weight of your body as you now recall or imagine the kindnesses happening to you in this very moment: the farmers who grew the food you're eating for lunch, texts from a friend, help from a colleague, the earth for providing air and sunshine or rain, birds singing outside your window. Imagine whoever made the chair you're sitting on and the clothes you're wearing.

6. Still breathing and paying attention to your feet and the weight of your body, offer appreciation and gratitude to yourself, to all the beings you thought about during this meditation, and to all those you didn't remember. You might give a blessing like, "May we all be safe and happy" or silently say, "I offer my gratitude to all beings for their love and care."

7. Finally, as you conclude this meditation, take a few deep breaths, pay attention to your feet and the weight of your body, and stretch or move. Remember, you can call your Lineage of Kindness at any time, wherever you are, and whenever you need help and support.

CHAPTER 9

When You're Too Sad to Move

For most people the struggle is the daily-ness, that's where the heartbreak lies. That's what grief looks like most of the time: today it's going to be hard to make a cup of tea.

—Aisling Bea[1]

SHAUN'S BELOVED GRANDMOTHER WAS NINETY-SIX YEARS OLD, BED-ridden, and dying. She didn't have a particular ailment or illness, but as she liked to say, she was "wearing out"—her body was frail and she was so tired she slept most of the time. She lived with Shaun's mom in their family home outside of Chicago. Shaun worked long hours as a dispatch manager for a commercial shipping company near O'Hare Airport and lived in an apartment near his office. But when his grandma could no longer walk and needed full-time care, Shaun, his mom, and his sister decided they would care for her at home, and for the next eight months, Shaun spent most evenings and weekends at her house. He didn't mind—he loved his grandma and it was nice to be with his family—but it was tiring, and he missed being able to watch the White Sox and the Bulls. Instead, he got home after ten at night, just in time to take a quick shower and go to sleep before another day of work.

He did this for eight months, until his grandma died peacefully in her bed, a few days after telling them that it was time for her to go and that they should not be sad. After the funeral, Shaun missed his grandma but he was also relieved. It was great to play basketball with his friends on Sundays again, and he resumed running after work, training for a 5K race. He spent more time with his daughter, who was in her third year at University of Illinois, Chicago, picking her up at the El and taking her to brunch at Poor Phil's near his house or to his mom's for dinner. His mother offered him his grandma's desk, a beat-up, decades-old rolltop, which he put in his living room under a window, where it reminded him of her.

But in the autumn, about a month after she died, Shaun's alarm rang at 6:00 a.m. as it always did, but he was so tired he could barely get up for work. The days dragged. His colleagues reminded him about meetings—twice about a drivers' meeting and still he forgot it, walking in ten minutes late apologizing. When he got home, he went straight to bed, got up a few hours later, microwaved frozen Korean pork buns, ate potato chips and a bowl of coffee ice cream, and got into bed with his laptop where he watched a few episodes of *The Shield* before going back to sleep. Each day was the same, although on the weekends he often got dinner delivered and even sometimes ate in bed.

> Pay close attention to yourself if you're feeling depressed. If the feelings last beyond a couple of weeks, be sure to talk to your doctor. If you have thoughts of suicide, serious weight loss, or can't work or perform normal duties for more than a day or two, you must seek professional help. Contact your doctor immediately and consider contacting the Substance Abuse and Mental Health Services Administration (SAMHSA) or the other organizations listed in the Resources section at the end of this book.

Shaun didn't really feel bad—just weary and a little bit numb. It never occurred to him that he was grieving or that the way he felt related to his grandmother's death. Since the weather was cooler and it was getting darker earlier, he figured it was normal to start to hibernate at home, like an animal preparing for winter. He hadn't seen his daughter in a few months, but she was busy with a new semester and he knew they'd be together at Thanksgiving, so he was surprised when she stopped by unexpectedly on a Sunday morning. She hugged him when she entered and looked around his apartment quizzically saying, "Dad, you look terrible. When was the last time you took a shower?"

Shaun was annoyed because he'd just showered a few days before—wasn't that enough?—but he said, "I'm fine, just a little tired with the time change and work." He sat down and turned on the television as she collected dishes from the coffee table and picked up his shoes from the floor. He could hear her cleaning up in the kitchen and called to her to leave that stuff alone and he'd get it later, but she didn't respond and turned on the dishwasher and took the garbage out the back door to the alley. When she returned, she sat down next to him on the couch. "Dad, I think you're depressed." Shaun felt sincerely surprised and a little bit confused as he replied, "I've never been depressed in my life!"

A common element of grief is depression. Clinicians suggest that when we feel the reality of our loss—when it sinks in that our loved one is really gone or that we'll never live in our old house again—signs of depression like fatigue, eating too much or too little, crying often, and/or difficulty sleeping may arise. We might feel lonely, empty, anxious, or like nothing really matters. The difference between grief-related depression and clinical depression is that the former usually resolves with time and support, whereas the latter might be long-lasting and require psychological treatment like therapy or medication to resolve. In Shaun's case, when he realized his daughter was right, he was able to allow himself to grieve and let his family support him through the process, checking on him daily, bringing him meals, and not nagging or pushing him to do anything or feel differently than he did. A few months later, on New Year's Day, he felt as if a weight had lifted from his chest for the first time in months and enjoyed watching the Rose Bowl with his nephews while helping his sister cook his grandmother's ham recipe for dinner.

If you're sleeping or crying a lot, aren't taking pleasure in anything, or are feeling overwhelmed by simple tasks like making coffee, you might be experiencing grief-related depression. If so, that's okay. There isn't one way to grieve—it's a process during which you have many different feelings and moods, and it's nonlinear, which means you might feel good for a while and then sad, depressed, overwhelmed, or anxious before you feel okay again. This difficult time can be an opportunity to bring all your kindness—all the patience, care, and generosity you share with others—to yourself.

In the Buddhist tradition, true love, compassion, and wisdom are impartial or indiscriminate—that is, we extend these qualities to everyone. And everyone includes us. The practice of self-compassion while you're depressed and grieving is to treat yourself with sensitivity and gentleness. Don't push or berate yourself or feel bad that you're not doing things that you think you should do right now. Instead, treat yourself as you would if you had a bad bout of the flu or another physical illness—giving yourself time to heal and recover by resting, relaxing, and being patient.

Notice if you're avoiding your support network—friends, family, or colleagues who care about you—and make an effort to connect with them. Researchers have found that depressed, grieving people who allow themselves to be cared for are more likely to gradually move on and resolve their feelings than those who don't.

In Buddhism, wisdom means acting in the most skillful way to alleviate suffering. During your period of grief, use your wisdom to alleviate your own suffering with compassion, tenderness, and deep friendship.

Sometimes people come to spiritual or religious practice with the expectation that they can use it to avoid suffering or unpleasantness. You'll sometimes hear people say, "I never feel upset anymore; God takes all my troubles," or "When I feel angry, I just use my mindfulness practice and change it to compassion." But there's truly no way to avoid physical or mental suffering or loss, and real spiritual practice means embracing all aspects of humanness with the grace of God or the support of our own wisdom and compassion.

About a decade ago, I was feeling disappointed in myself because I was still angry about being treated badly by a Zen teacher. I kept telling myself that I should get over it and that a "real" Buddhist would see how insignificant and "empty" my feelings about it were and let them go. And then I went on a weekend retreat and mentioned this to a different teacher, one I hardly knew at all. He was from the Korean Zen tradition and offered me this story to remind me of the relational nature of our lives and the unavoidable truth of loss and grief:

> A Zen teacher's grandchild died. Her students attended the funeral ceremonies and were surprised to discover she was grieving and bereft. One student, gathering his courage, blurted, "But how can you be so upset? You're a Zen master!" And she replied firmly, "Yes, I am a Zen master. But first I am a grandmother."

Practice 9: Just Breathe

Sometimes, we're so tired or depressed that the very most we can do is breathe. When you have moments like this, it's best to just allow yourself to rest. Don't push yourself, and don't expect to feel differently than you feel right now. Instead, notice all your judgments about yourself and any wishes you might have to feel differently, let them be, and rest in what is arising right now. We often think of rest or relaxation as a moment when our mind is free from thoughts or difficult feelings. But real relaxation occurs when we're not trying to make anything be different than it is. We can simply stop, do nothing, and rest—in sadness, joy, depression, pain, and ease—without clinging to pleasantness, pushing away unpleasantness, or ignoring dullness.

1. Find someplace where you don't have to hold yourself up—a chair, the floor, a bed, a couch—somewhere you don't have to make any physical effort at all. Let your body settle here, and don't worry that you should be doing something—you are doing something. You're taking care of yourself.

2. Put your hand on your belly, and let it move with the rise and fall of your inhalations and exhalations. You don't have to fix or change your breath. There is nothing wrong, so nothing needs to be fixed or corrected. Just let yourself be, and when you get caught up in a regret or a worry or an opinion, gently return your attention to your breath and let yourself sink into your seat. With each exhalation, you can let yourself drop a bit deeper into your seat and the earth. You can let yourself be without expecting to be different or to feel differently than you're feeling right now.

3. As you rest, you can silently say to yourself with each breath, "I'm here for you." You can breathe into any vulnerable places, tight spots, or scared parts of you and reassure yourself quietly, saying: *I am here for you. You're not alone.* Or try saying, *I'm really struggling right now, and it's okay. This is a moment of suffering. May I be open to my suffering. I allow the earth to hold me up.* Or, *Oh dear one, you are really having a hard time and I hear you.* You can use any or all of these phrases or make up your own.

4. The most important instruction right now is to be kind, patient, and friendly to your pain, sadness, grief, worry, tiredness—whatever you're feeling is okay. Grief unfolds naturally and you don't have to push it away or control it, only give yourself permission to acknowledge it and allow it with compassion and love.

CHAPTER 10

Complicated Relationships, Complicated Grief

Dear lovely Death,
Change is thy other name
—LANGSTON HUGHES[1]

AFTER MY MOM'S FUNERAL IN WISCONSIN, MY FRIENDS LORI AND Denise drove me to Chicago where they lived. I'd booked a flight from O'Hare back to New York City the next morning and was eager to get home. I missed my cats, who were kindly being tended by my next-door neighbor, Neil, and I looked forward to seeing Paul, the funny sci-fi writer I'd only started dating a month before. I was in the middle of an intensive meditation teacher training program and excited to return to my practice and study.

At Denise's apartment that afternoon, I folded my laundry in her robin's-egg blue guest bedroom as Iver, her fat tabby cat, jumped in and out of the luggage sitting open on the bed. I suddenly felt such a sinking sensation that I sat down on the floor and looked out the window into the dimming late summer light and thought, "I don't feel right." I got up and found Denise at her dining room table, spreading OxiClean on the old, embroidered dishcloths we found in my mom's kitchen that Denise thought were vintage and fun and I thought were cheap and kitschy. I told her I wasn't feeling right, and she suggested a shower might help. As I stood beneath the warm water, I didn't feel better—and in fact became overwhelmed with fear. My body trembled, my heart raced, and my stomach was hot and tight. I knew I was having a panic attack but I couldn't understand why—*I'd been sure that the only thing I'd feel after my mom died was relief.* Our relationship had been so unpleasant and painful that it didn't occur to me that I would suffer any loss at all. But the death of a parent or any important loss— like the end of a marriage, intimate relationship, or friendship—even a bad one—is always a profound and painful psychological shock, no matter how complicated or difficult it may have been.

If a difficult relationship ends and your grief is destabilizing, causes insomnia, paranoia, intrusive thoughts, or you find yourself unable to cope with your day-to-day life, you could be experiencing a psychological condition called *complicated grief*. Consider psychotherapy, pastoral guidance, or formal grief counseling, and check out the organizations in the Resources section at the end of this book.

My mom always felt like a burden I needed to carry. Growing up, she was an unreliable, needy alcoholic. I learned early how to manage her feelings and try to take care of both of our needs. Throughout my adulthood, I alternated between feeling resentful of her dependency on me, enraged by all her bad decisions that I had to help clean up, and guilty for not being the good and loving daughter she wanted. When her health declined a few years before her death, I reeled with frustration and helplessness while she continued to drink and smoke despite her struggles with chronic obstructive pulmonary disease and emphysema. It was during this time that I realized I would be relieved when she died. Even though I didn't wish her dead and truly wanted her to be happy and not to suffer, I looked forward to freedom from the responsibility of being her daughter and only relative.

I thought of this while I stood in the shower at Denise's place and realized although I *was* glad to not have to take care of my mom anymore, I was affected by her death. However troubled our relationship had been, it was still a relationship, and she was still my mom. Her death was—like it or not—a great and painful loss that would take time for me to understand and process.

I stayed in the robin's-egg blue room for another week, afraid to be alone as I struggled with intrusive thoughts. I was grateful that Lori and Denise were happy to take care of me, and it was comfortable and healing to spend time with them and my niece Madeleine. I cooked dinner every night, and when they got done with work, we sat around Denise's too-tall glass dining table and I served my favorite turkey meatball recipe one night and baked cauliflower mac and cheese another. We drank wine while listening to Denise's favorite old Burt Bacharach albums and I felt relieved, safe, and relaxed.

It didn't last. When I returned to my apartment in New York, my panic attacks intensified. The death of my mom compounded with living alone and by the normal stress of work and school made me feel worse. The only time I felt at ease was during brief moments with friends, while I was at yoga class, or when I was practicing at the meditation center. Alone at home I had night terrors several times a week, awakening in my bed sweaty and afraid at three in the morning—the same time that my mom had died. After dark, my anxiety escalated, and on some nights, Lori even stayed on the phone with me while I fell asleep.

I thought it would end soon enough and that I wasn't doing that bad and didn't want to seek professional help. But one brisk morning just before Thanksgiving, after I zipped up my fleece jacket, grabbed my rolled-up mat, and opened the door to leave the yoga studio, I heard my teacher Cassandra call out to me, "Wait! You forgot your shoes!" I stopped on the threshold and looked down at my cold bare feet, incredulous, and turned around. Cassandra said to me kindly, "Kim, you're really ungrounded right now," and as I put my sneakers on, I realized I needed support.

At the recommendation of a friend who was part of my meditation community, I visited Athena, a somatic healer in Brooklyn. She suggested I was experiencing a trauma response—the death of my mom had reopened many deep wounds of abandonment and abuse, which were causing anxiety attacks and fear. She suggested zero balancing, a gentle form of acupressure, and treated me in the spare room of her garden apartment overlooking a birdbath. These sessions alleviated some of the disassociation I'd been experiencing, and I supplemented them by reading books about the loss of a parent and the grieving process, which helped me understand how hard it is for everyone. One Sunday I took the train to the Tibetan monastery in Duchess County where I studied and talked to Lama Wangmo, a Buddhist nun. She encouraged me to treat myself with great patience and kindness and not to think of my panic attacks as something *other* than myself that I needed to get rid of, but instead to see them as my own misplaced energy. Finally, I sought the guidance of a psychotherapist too. When I met Lynne in her comfortable and tiny Upper West Side office, she explained that the clinical term for what I was experiencing was complicated grief.

Complicated grief often occurs after the end of intimate relationships that were abusive, painful, hurtful, or destructive. It often surprises us, because most of us believe we'll only feel good when bad relationships like these end. Indeed, leaving an abusive husband or separating from a controlling and demanding partner is seen as healthy and empowering—what's to feel bad about? My former colleague Jean said as much when we had lunch near her office a month or two after my mom's death. "Well, I'm glad you don't have to deal with that mess anymore," she said when our skinny margaritas arrived.

"Now you can put it all behind you and relax." Unfortunately, it's not that easy. Complicated grieving reveals an unsettling truth: troubled intimate relationships don't end when the person dies or the divorce is final. They end when our thoughts and feelings about our experiences with them are compassionately recognized and understood.

When Robert's wife Ann left, he too felt a sense of relief—he was finally at peace in his own home. But soon he felt heavy and heartbroken. He'd met Ann when they both worked as fundraisers for their church. They seemed to have so much in common: a love of God and community and both were excellent swing dancers. After less than a year of dating, they married, and Robert knew immediately he'd made a mistake. Ann was jealous to the point of reading his emails and unlocking his phone, misinterpreting messages from friends and even his mother as threats against her and their marriage. When he was with Ann, he was always on the defensive or trying to reassure her. At first, he felt sorry for her because he could see that she was genuinely upset and he hoped she could feel more secure if he were patient and as their life together became more familiar. But she couldn't control her anger and refused the pastor's invitation for couples' counseling, and soon Robert spent as much time as he could at work or the gym, often stopping at his mom's house on the way home, where they would sit quietly and watch *Empire* on television together. When Ann abruptly left close to three years after they married and moved in with a divorced man she'd recently met at her bowling league, Robert was surprised by how upset he was—unable to sleep and sure that his friends and family thought he was a fool—until he spoke with Pastor Charles. They met weekly to explore Robert's grief at being left single again in middle age and his reasons for missing his unpredictable and untrustworthy ex-wife.

After a few months, Robert realized that when he lost his spouse, he also lost the possibility of having a better relationship with her; it was hard to let go of this deeply felt wish. Similarly, I'd hoped for so long—my entire life—that my mom would stop drinking and become a supportive and loving presence, just as Robert wished for a happy marriage. When my mom died, I was able to mourn my longing and recognize how truly sad it was that she and I would never be close— sad for me and sad for her, too. And when Robert realized his broken heart was as much for his yearning for true love and connection as it was for the end of his marriage, he felt freer to let go of his ex-wife and begin again with another person.

If you go to a museum and look at the art from Asia, you might notice statues of the Buddha holding a large, smooth, oval-shaped object in front of his heart. This is the *Chintamani*, or wish-fulfilling gem. It's described in this old Buddhist parable:

A woman from the city visits her old friend, who is quite wealthy. The city woman stays at her friend's large estate in the country for several weeks, and both are glad to spend such a pleasant time in good company together. Before the city woman leaves, the wealthy woman asks her maid to secretly sew a priceless jewel into the hem of her friend's black coat. She knows her friend would not accept such an extravagant gift and it makes her happy to give her friend something that could help her if she were ever in need.

Many years pass, and the friends' lives have moved in different directions for the usual reasons—commitments, marriages, and children—and they've lost touch with one another. One day, the wealthy woman is at the market and notices a beggar on the sidewalk asking for money. She stops to make an offering and realizes the disheveled person in a tattered black coat is her old friend. She sits down next to her and asks, "What happened? Didn't you find the gem sewn into your coat?" The city woman touches the hem, finds the jewel and says, "I didn't know it was here."

We all carry a priceless gem with us—it's our own true nature, our limitless capacity for wisdom and compassion for ourselves and others. Most of us live like the city woman— unaware that we possess it. But we can trust that even in the darkest times when we might feel bereft, confused, or wounded, we can find our own Chintamani and fulfill our wish to be healthy, healed, happy, and connected.

Practice 10: Meditation in Motion

Although I'd been meditating for years, when my mom died, I was unable to be quiet and still. Whenever I sat down to practice, I was restless and shaky and my thoughts proliferated like wildfire. I couldn't focus on my breath or the sounds around me, and on several occasions, I sat down in my meditation seat and suddenly found myself at the sink getting a glass of water—I'd stopped meditating and walked from the living room to the kitchen so lost in stories and anxiety that I didn't even realize I'd moved.

The Buddha taught that there are four postures conducive to contemplative practice—sitting, standing, lying down, and walking. All are useful ways to develop insight, concentration, and compassion. I'd learned walking meditation during retreats at the Insight Meditation Society in Barre, Massachusetts, and it seemed like a good time to begin doing it in my apartment. I lived in an old tenement and the space was small—I could take only a dozen or so unobstructed steps down my hallway before I had to turn around—but it didn't matter. Moving helped calm me and feeling my feet on the floor shifted me out of my head and into my body, making me feel less disconnected and more real.

If you feel too overwhelmed to practice sitting meditation, you can try walking practice. It doesn't require equipment or props, and you can do it anywhere—in a tiny jail cell, on a quiet country road, at the beach, in your backyard, or on the sidewalk outside your office. There are many types of walking meditation—the Zen tradition has slow walking and fast walking—but what works best for me is to walk at a steady, relaxed pace, to keep my hands resting gently at my sides, and to concentrate all my attention on the soles of my feet. It's easiest to do barefoot but if that's not possible, make sure your shoes are comfortable.

Remember, if you're unable to walk, you can still use your body to center your mind and calm your nervous system. Try lying down on the couch or the floor and rest all your attention on the back of your body. Sense your shoulder blades, thighs, and heels. Notice how they're touching the fabric or floor, and on each exhalation, see if you can let yourself relax a little bit more. If you get distracted, it's okay, just start again—and again.

1. Begin by standing if you can. Put your hand on your belly and feel it move as you make five deep inhalations and full exhalations. Tuck your tailbone and stand up straight as you relax your shoulders. Notice the air around you. Just stay here for a minute or so and breathe.

2. Take your first step. Without looking, feel your leg lifting and moving through space and feel both feet as they're placed on the floor. Experience the sensations of your heel, then the balls of your feet, and finally all five of your toes as they touch the earth.

3. Continue steps 1 and 2. Don't look around—let your gaze fall to the ground in front of you or look straight ahead—your attention isn't with the sensation of sight but rather the feeling of your feet. Let yourself relax and feel how gravity holds you securely to the earth. If your thoughts about tomorrow sweep you into a story or fantasy, that's okay. Choose to gently move your attention from your head to your feet again and again.

This is a very simple practice but it might seem complicated and hard to concentrate at first. It might not even feel like meditation since there's so much movement. But if you patiently keep walking and directing your focus to your feet, you'll feel a shift away from your thoughts to the direct experience of your body. You'll notice that even when thoughts arise, they don't have to dominate your awareness. You can choose to relax into the safety of your body and the wisdom of being a living creature on the earth.

CHAPTER 11

Grieving for Strangers

Our lives are not our own. We are bound to others, past and present, and by each crime and every kindness, we birth our future.
—DAVID MITCHELL[1]

WHEN THE EAST COAST OF THE UNITED STATES EXPERIENCED A record-breaking storm, the aftereffects of Hurricane Ida, which had devastated the Gulf Coast, New York City received the most rainfall in the shortest period of time in history, causing widespread damage and flash flooding throughout the area. Cars stalled on highways in waist-deep water, torrents of rain overwhelmed and closed the subway system, and every basement in town flooded. In my neighborhood of Jackson Heights, Queens, many apartment buildings suffered catastrophic damage, and the day after the storm volunteers helped pump basements and remove damaged furniture and belongings. We learned of several injuries and a few fatalities, including a local family. Mingma Sherpa and Ang Gelu Lama and their two-year-old son, Lobsang, lived in a basement apartment in a small three-family flat not far from the subway station. Their unit had only one entrance, and when water suddenly cascaded down the steps and to their door and poured into their windows, it quickly filled their home. With no way to escape, they drowned. I imagined their horror and fear as they fought to get out of the building, as they struggled to hold on to their little boy and each other, and as they were overcome by the powerful floodwaters rushing against them. Thinking of their panic and confusion, I felt deeply sad and sat down on a bench and cried.

> "Paying attention" is not the same as watching the news or reading social media or doomscrolling. It's choosing to make a real connection to others through your mind and heart. The next time you read or hear about a tragedy, shut off your device, close your eyes, and sit still for a few moments as you notice how you might be affected. Then offer your love and wisdom to all who were harmed.

In our modern lives, we regularly see photographs and videos of tragic events from around the world, and our hearts are touched daily by what we see on television, the internet, and social media. We don't have to know people personally to grieve their death or feel their anguish, and most of us in the United States have experienced a collective sense of mourning many times. In the past decade alone, the country grieved when eleven people were massacred at a Pittsburgh synagogue, when forty-nine people were killed in a mass shooting at the Pulse nightclub in Florida, when Hurricane Michael destroyed parts of Florida and Georgia, when more than seven hundred thousand people died from COVID-19, and when George Floyd was murdered.

Mr. Floyd's death is a powerful example of how we connect to a stranger's tragedy because it was captured on video and widely shared. Millions of people watched as he was arrested, thrown to the ground, and handcuffed by the police. While Mr. Floyd lay helpless, face down on the pavement, Derek Chauvin, a police officer, proudly knelt on Mr. Floyd's neck and back as he struggled beneath him, clearly in distress and unable to breathe. Despite Mr. Floyd's pleas, Derek Chauvin posed atop him, and dozens of bystanders yelled at Chauvin to get up, begging him to stop killing the man. It's terrifying to see and hear his suffering and to feel the helplessness of the witnesses who were prevented from intervening by other police officers. And it's utterly heartbreaking to hear Mr. Floyd say his last words, "I can't breathe," and then fall still. This barbaric act of cruelty, racism, and ignorance brought deep sadness and grief to many Americans, who were filled with anger, shame, and sorrow for Mr. Floyd, the Black community, and the country itself.

When we allow ourselves to feel the loss and suffering of any individual, it reminds us of the wisdom of our shared humanity—that all our lives are brief, precious, and vulnerable, and everyone is helpless in the face of suffering. We grieve because we know that we too will grow older, get sick, lose what we love, and die, because this is the reality of our lives. These poignant facts include not only humans but animals too—which is why the Buddhist tradition emphasizes our connection with *all* living beings. We're encouraged to develop our insight and compassion not only for ourselves but for everyone because of this deep connection.

Growing up, I was taught to love and care for only a limited group of humans and animals. This included my family, close friends, our pets, and maybe some special people like the pope or Martin Luther King Jr. and special animals like dolphins and elephants. But I was rarely encouraged to consider the other vast majority of living creatures, and some—like insects or flawed or dangerous people—I was told it was okay to despise and feel no compassion for them at all. That's because I—like so many of us—hadn't learned to pay attention, so I didn't see our shared struggles or our interdependence, so I couldn't respond to their struggles, except sometimes with pity or denial. When I began studying Buddhism, I was surprised and inspired by my teachers, who explained that we could all develop our compassion indiscriminately and boundlessly—and share it with not only ourselves and our close circle, but also with strangers, people we don't like, frightening insects, and even dangerous beings like vicious dogs and murderers.

As I practiced enlarging my circle of care, I connected to my own difficulties. I realized I'd also been pitying and denying my sadness, loss, and anger, and I learned to pay attention to all my experiences with patience, to accept that all lives have struggles and imperfections, and I was no exception. I noticed that everyone, everywhere, experiences difficulties and suffers. This is the nature of things.

When we mourn the death and pain of strangers, we're acknowledging our shared experience, letting them know and reminding ourselves that they're neither forgotten nor alone. As we keep our loving attention on them, our hearts and minds are prepared to act or speak skillfully for their benefit when we are able. Recognizing the sorrows of strangers inspires us to create conditions that alleviate suffering and bring solace, compassion, and wisdom to strangers and to everyone—knowing that even if we can't make immediate changes, our actions can influence change in the future.

The Buddhist intention to benefit all beings is the great vow of the bodhisattva—an inspirational, idealized being who alleviates the suffering of the world. Buddhist students aspire to become bodhisattvas by devoting our practice—words, deeds, and thoughts—to being of benefit and doing no harm. This is called the path of the bodhisattva and it's a joyful way to live.

Orienting your life to benefit the world is an antidote for the greed and isolation many of us feel and an encouragement to remember the courage and love possible in all our human hearts. Because we are inspired by our work and recognize the potential for an equitable, peaceful world for all, aspiring bodhisattvas do their best to connect with as many beings as possible—directly and indirectly. You don't have to take a formal vow or even be a Buddhist to become an aspiring bodhisattva. All you need to do is use your thoughts, speech, and behavior wisely and mindfully, knowing that even if you can't prevent all suffering—war, racism, poverty, confusion, disasters—you can use your actions to create new causes and conditions that alleviate suffering in the future. Aspiring bodhisattvas don't worry about changing the world immediately and instead take a long view, understanding that although we might not see differences in our lifetimes, the outcome of our beneficial actions continues to affect the world even after we die.

Practice 11: Awake to the World

Although most of us have been taught to conserve our emotional energy and limit our care and love to our family and friends, we can learn to expand it to all living creatures. An easy way to do this is to notice our natural instinct to be generous, kind, and attentive to those we already know and to develop and expand these qualities to include people we like, people we don't like, strangers, and nonhumans.

With this simple *metta* meditation, you're encouraged to appreciate and honor your beautiful qualities, widen your circle of care, and open your boundless heart to everyone.

1. Shut off your devices. Find a quiet spot, get still, stop talking, and put your hand on your heart. Take a few breaths.

2. Imagine someone you love and care about who might be struggling. Repeat silently as if speaking to them, *May you be free from danger, violence, and hatred. May your actions bring benefit and do no harm.* Continue this for five or more minutes.

3. Now visualize yourself, and repeat silently, *May I be free from danger, violence, and hatred. May my actions bring benefit and do no harm.* Continue this for five or more minutes.

4. Take a moment to honor your intentions and all the wisdom and kindness you've shared with your loved one and yourself during this practice. You can say thank you to yourself or simply acknowledge your appreciation for your generosity and goodness.

5. Now imagine yourself, your loved one, and a stranger or group of strangers who have recently experienced tragedy. You might

visualize all of you in the same room or standing together hold-ing hands. Repeat silently, *May all of us be free from danger, vio-lence, and hatred. May all our actions bring benefit and do no harm.*

6. Before you conclude your meditation, take a moment to acknowledge your efforts and thank yourself.

CHAPTER 12

Beloved Pets

We're not, after all, separate from the animal kingdom. We're part of it.

—Jane Goodall[1]

For more than twenty years, I lived with my sweet cat, Simone. I adopted her when I was a college student living near Wrigley Field in Chicago. My ex-boyfriend Rob's mom told us about an animal rescuer who lived uptown right off Lake Michigan in Andersonville, and he drove us there on a rainy night in his tiny old Ford Escort. We parked in front of an old bungalow in need of repair and were greeted at the door by a middle-aged woman in a flannel shirt and jeans, straining to hold the collar of a wildly barking terrier while shouting for us to hurry inside. The rambling house was filled with cats and a few dogs, and when we walked into the kitchen, we met Simone—a shy, small, young, entirely black female cat. She wasn't sure she trusted humans, which attracted me to her because I felt the same way. When I brought her home that night, she promptly hid under the couch until two days later, when she crept into bed and snuggled next to me just before dawn.

Simone lived with me for the next two decades, through several long-term relationships and jobs, sharing my successes and delights at school and with friends. The responsibility of caring for her helped me make a home for both of us as we learned to feel safe and loved. During the last years of her life, she had kidney disease and one cold day in December when she was twenty-one years old, she could no longer walk and refused to eat. Dr. Ted, our vet, said her suffering would only get worse and that it was time for euthanasia. Cradling her in her favorite blanket in a quiet treatment room at Dr. Ted's office, he gave her an injection and she stopped breathing. I felt my heart sink and immediately thought desperately, "Oh no, come back, Simone, come back," but she was dead, and I painfully understood the profound irrevocability of death as I cried.

> Although your employer or school might not honor pet bereavement with time off or excused absences, you can still treat yourself with tenderness and kindness while you process your loss. Be sure to be patient and gentle with yourself during moments of sadness or loneliness. Call a friend, light a candle, sit quietly with your hand on your heart, and don't be embarrassed to ask for help from your family or a support group.

For the next few months, I acutely felt Simone's absence, and waves of sadness washed over me unexpectedly—in the subway, at work, and especially in our home. I could almost see a hole in the spaces where she used to be—her bed next to the radiator, the place beside me on the bed, the cushion on the couch, the toys in the hall-way. When I went with my boyfriend to his best friend's birthday party in March, I still didn't feel like myself and didn't really want to go. Many of his friends were sports fans and I didn't have much in common with them. I felt annoyed when we walked in and everyone was cheering the Knicks on television. I was surprised when, returning from the bathroom, I heard my boyfriend mention to his friend James, a triathlete who worked for Major League Baseball, that my cat had died. Expecting James to nod with indifference, I was surprised when he said, "Oh, no wonder she's upset. We have two cats and they're part of our family, we'd be lost without them."

Nearly eighty-five million families in the United States— 67 percent—have at least one pet, and as any pet owner knows, our connection with these animals is as real as any human relationship, because dogs and cats—not to mention other creatures like horses, mice, and elephants—form authentic bonds of trust and kindness with humans. So it's understandable and normal that the death of a beloved pet would cause us sadness, grief, and mourning.

This surprised Isa. After Robinson, her family dog died, she didn't expect to feel the loss. He was her children's pet, a golden retriever mutt adopted from an animal shelter when he was six months old and her kids were four and six. But five years later, after she and her husband separated and he got his own place, Isa noticed that Robinson took on a new role. In the past he had spent the night on her son's bed and stayed there until she got up and fed him in the morning, but now he patrolled the house at night, seemingly ensuring their safety, and took turns sleeping in all three of their beds. He seemed to know when the kids were sad or uneasy or when they felt upset with their parents, because during those times Robinson would be sure to sit next to them on the couch or join them on a walk to the park. When he was ten, he was struck by a car and killed. Isa's children grieved and she did too—because she realized he was not just an animal, but a truly important member of their family.

One thing pets offer that we might not experience with humans is unconditional love. Pets don't have expectations that we be smart or get good grades or look great or be successful. They love us as we are and are generally eager and happy to see us. I'd never experienced being loved in such an easy way before I met Simone, and her steady, reliable, and consistent attachment helped me heal, taught me that I could trust myself to be a caring and responsible person and that I was loveable no matter what I looked like, did for a living, or opinions I held.

In Buddhism, our unconditional love is not reserved solely for humans but is a quality that is extended to all beings. Buddhist students learn to develop *metta* (loving-kindness) impartially for ourselves, our family and friends, strangers, animals, fish, birds—all living creatures on earth. This *metta* arises from the wisdom that, just like us, other creatures feel suffering and the knowledge that our lives affect all other lives because all creatures rely on each other in our interdependent ecosystem called earth.

Grieving a beloved pet is an opportunity to recognize our boundless capacity to love without discrimination and our deep connection with all beings. We can transform our loss into an appreciation for life and rejoice in the possibility of everyone on the planet living together harmoniously with genuine peace and kindness.

Traditional Buddhists believe in reincarnation or continual rebirth—that we've all lived many lifetimes as many different creatures. It's believed that we've all died and been born as cats, dogs, insects, humans, fish, and birds. Because we've done this so many times, we've all encountered each other before. The early teachings say, "A being who has not been your mother at one time in the past is not easy to find. . . . [A] being who has not been your father . . . your brother . . . your sister . . . your son . . . your daughter at one time in the past is not easy to find."

I don't actually believe in reincarnation, but I was surprised by my reaction to a centipede a few months after my dear friend Denise died. It appeared in my bathtub, and although I have no phobia of insects, they disgust and frighten me, and I quickly stepped away from the tub, wondering if I should splash water toward it to encourage it to leave. Then I thought, "What if that's Denise?" Suddenly I felt protective and concerned. I cared about a centipede! I closed the bathroom door to prevent my cats from entering and harming it and insisted my husband not kill it or bother it. I finally understood why my teachers emphasized reincarnation—because it doesn't matter whether reincarnation is "real" or not—what matters is that it helps us to regard any living creature as a friend, and in so doing we can dramatically expand our circle of love and care to include everyone in the world.

Practice 12: Appreciation

Practicing gratitude is a way to appreciate what's valuable to us and offers a means of balancing the sorrows and the joys of our lives. After the death or loss of anyone we love—including a beloved pet—we can take time to remember moments of joy and kindness we shared together, to focus not only on the pain of our grief, but on the delight of our connection. Offering appreciation gives us a way to recognize the impermanence of our relationships, and to value both those we have and those we've lost. Here are a few useful exercises to generate gratitude when you're mourning.

1. Keep a daily gratitude journal. Psychologists say practicing gratitude is the single easiest way to feel happier, and when you're bereaved it's important to balance your suffering and loss with your blessings and support. Every day, write down three things you're grateful to have. Make sure each day's list is different. It can include people, places, things, or moments. A recent entry in my gratitude journal says, "Today I'm grateful for the farmers who grew the apples in the apple cobbler I had for dessert, my sweet cat Simone who died and whose love and affection helped heal my fears of not being a good and reliable person, and my favorite old sneakers that make my feet feel comfortable."

2. Contemplate joy. You can do this exercise anytime you feel stuck or overwhelmed with sadness. Find a quiet spot to sit, close your eyes, and let yourself remember moments of recent joy in your life. Allow your mind to wander through the past month or so. You might remember peacefully resting in bed and hearing the rain, laughing with your granddaughter on the

telephone, beaming with happiness that your son got a promotion, feeling delight that your team won, or enjoying a meal at your favorite restaurant. When you've finished, put your hand on your heart and say, "I'm glad I can experience joy."

3. Practice gratitude meditation. Find a quiet spot to sit, turn off your devices, close your eyes, and take a few deep breaths. After a few minutes, think of your deceased pet or another being you've lost and are mourning. You might imagine them or simply feel a connection to them. Silently say to them, *I offer gratitude for your life. I offer gratitude for your kindness. May you be at peace.* Take a few minutes to repeat these kind and wise words as if you're offering a blessing. If you lose the connection or start thinking of something else, it's okay. Just come back to your breath, reconnect with your loved one, and start the phrases again. When you're ready, you can let go of this connection and take a few breaths and notice whatever is arising.

4. Make a connection with yourself. You can imagine yourself as a child or feel your presence as you give yourself these same wise and kind words: *I offer gratitude for all life. I offer gratitude for all kindness. May I be at peace.* Take your time and keep repeating these blessings as if you're giving yourself a gift. Remember, if your mind wanders off, it's okay, come back to your breath, reconnect, and begin again. Take your time, and after five minutes or so, you can let go of this connection to yourself, breathe, and notice whatever is arising.

5. Finally, take a moment to recognize everyone, all the beings on earth who experience joys and sorrows, just like us. Say silently, *May all beings offer gratitude for life. May we offer gratitude for kindness. May we be at peace.* When you conclude the meditation, be sure to thank yourself and appreciate your efforts.

CHAPTER 13

Divorce

It's sad, something coming to an end. It cracks you open, in a way—cracks you open to feeling. When you try to avoid the pain, it creates greater pain.

—JENNIFER ANISTON[1]

Vijay was watching the documentary *An Inconvenient Truth* with Thomas, his partner of nearly five years, when Thomas said he wanted to talk. Vijay paused the movie. Thomas told Vijay he was moving out, asked Vijay to keep their cats for a while until he had a new home for them, then picked up the remote to resume the movie, and left the room. Vijay was stunned. A decade later and happily married, Vijay remembers that moment with painful clarity, including how stupid and worthless he felt then and for a long time afterward.

My mom had a similar experience. I was twelve when my father's friend Bill died, and my dad began an affair with Bill's widow, Jean. He kept it a secret for six months before finally leaving my mom and moving in with Jean and her children. My mom, already a troubled and traumatized person, was devastated. Her sense of self was destroyed. She felt ashamed and enraged about being deceived and divorced, and she held on to this for the rest of her life—nearly forty years.

The stress of divorce and separation can detrimentally impact emotional and physical health. Many studies indicate it can lower vitality, decrease social functioning, and even can contribute to heart disease and other chronic conditions. Be sure to monitor yourself regularly, checking in with your body and your emotions every day. Don't fight your feelings or think you need to get over anything right away. Even an amicable split can be sad and hard. Be sure to rely on your friends and family, and don't be afraid to reach out to a support group to remind yourself that you're not alone and that you'll make it through this, just as so many others have done too.

Divorce—including breakups of long-term partnerships—is among the most stressful life event we can experience, and the grief and mourning that follows can be as intense and painful as a death. With a breakup, everything changes—our home, our social life, and our family. We no longer have the person we depended on and trusted, and often we feel helpless and abandoned. Starting over alone or with another person might seem impossible, and on top of these normal feelings of loss, the end of a relationship is often complicated by internalized guilt, shame, and blame. This is why Vijay called himself a loser and didn't tell his sister about his breakup for months and why my mother felt too embarrassed to return to our family church, convinced everyone was staring at her with pity or judgment.

The Buddhist tradition has a metaphor to describe difficult circumstances like loss, death, and sickness. It's said that these circumstances are similar to being struck by an arrow—painful, serious, and in need of proper care to heal. Getting shot with life's arrows is unavoidable—all humans will face the inevitable pain of change and impermanence. But other arrows are avoidable. The complicated feelings that might arise from an injury, a failed business, or a divorce—insistence that it shouldn't be happening, shame, blame, and self-judgment—are called "second arrows." These are optional, but because of our habits, expectations, and conditioning, we often don't realize we've shot ourselves with a second arrow and are causing ourselves additional pain.

Sometimes we unknowingly inflict a second arrow to try to protect ourselves from feeling the raw, tender wound caused by the first arrow. If this happens, we might not be able to fully process our loss. My mom didn't understand it, but her rage at my father for leaving her—her second arrow—was a defense mechanism she created to protect herself. It helped her to avoid feelings of the heartbreak of abandonment and deep insecurity, but it also prevented her from processing her feelings and accepting change so she could move past the divorce and create a new life for herself. Vijay, with the help of a counselor and supportive friends, was able to recognize that his insistence on taking the entire blame for his failed marriage—his second arrow—enabled him to continue a lifelong pattern of overlooking his partners' faults because he was afraid to be alone. This defense mechanism prevented him from seeing Thomas's fear of commitment and inability to compromise, both of which contributed to the breakup. Once he understood this, he was able to reach his deep loneliness and offer himself comfort and healing.

It's important not to view the second arrow as bad, stupid, or wrong, because then we might use it against ourselves as further evidence of why *we* are bad, stupid, or wrong. The second arrows we inflict on ourselves are learned behaviors, but we can unlearn them with mindfulness and kindness. We can pay attention to the habitual ways we add to the difficulty of divorce, separation, and other painful life events—through shame, blame, anger, catastrophizing—and bring compassion to ourselves. We can offer patience and kindness to our pain as we attend to the underlying heartbreak—the first arrow—so we can properly restore ourselves and heal.

Buddhism encourages all of us to discover that we have a true home within ourselves and that we don't have to look outside to other people or gather material possessions to make us feel satisfied, loved, and happy. Instead, everyone can take "refuge" in their true home—their clear, wise, and kind mind—which we all possess and can access through mindfulness and skillful action.

Buddhists often take formal refuge vows, seeking protection in the truth of our self-reliance and putting our trust in our inherent worthiness. The traditional vows say, "I go to the Buddha as my refuge; I go to the *Dhamma* as my refuge; I go to the *Sangha* as my refuge." Here, the Buddha represents our own inherent wisdom, the *Dhamma* are methods to help us find it, and the *Sangha* are people on the path along with us. If you're not a Buddhist, you can recite similar vows to connect with your own true home, especially if you're feeling lost or abandoned. Put your hand on your heart and say to yourself, "I take refuge in my kind and open nature; I take refuge in activities that lead me to recognize my kind and open nature; I take refuge with others who support me in finding my kind and open nature."

Practice 13: Self-Compassion

Feelings of self-loathing, self-blame, shame, guilt, and self-critical thoughts can be so familiar and habitual that we don't even consciously notice them. This self-compassion practice helps you to open your heart to the pain of a breakup, separation, estrangement, or divorce and to alleviate the unnecessary suffering of these negative thoughts. In this *metta* (loving-kindness) meditation, you'll allow yourself to *receive* kindness, helping you soften harsh thoughts and meet struggles with self-compassion.

1. Find a quiet place where you won't be disturbed. You can sit or lie down—whatever is comfortable. Close your eyes and take several deep, slow inhalations and exhalations.

    After a few minutes, place your hand on your heart and call to mind a dear one—someone who has treated you in a loving and open way. Someone who believes you're a wonderful person and is always happy to see you. Refrain from using a sibling or parent because these relationships can be complicated. Instead, connect with an aunt, uncle, or grandparent, a close friend, therapist, teacher, or a pet. Visualize this dear one, imagining they are right there with you and feeling their presence beside you.

2. Now, silently repeat these phrases to this dear one: *May you be happy. May you be free from suffering. May you be at peace with the way things are.* Continue giving these blessings to the dear one silently for a few minutes, imagining you're offering them a gift.

3. After you finish saying the phrases, continue to connect with your dear one. Imagine they are looking directly into your eyes and are saying to you, *May you be happy. May you be free from*

suffering. May you be at peace with the way things are. Allow yourself to hear and receive these blessings from this dear one for several minutes or as long as you wish.

4. Continue imagining that your dear one is with you—perhaps standing next to you with a hand on your shoulder or you just sense their presence. And imagine you're looking at yourself in the mirror, noticing your struggles and suffering. Now offer yourself the same heartfelt blessings: *May I be happy. May I be free from suffering. May I be at peace with the way things are.*

5. Take your time with this practice. Spend as long as you like with each of the steps, giving your attention where you feel you need it the most.

CHAPTER 14

When You're Fired or Laid Off

There are opportunities even in the most difficult moments.
—Wangari Maathai[1]

Every month, nearly twenty million people in the United States are fired or involuntarily leave their jobs. But this truth—and the fact that everything changes—doesn't make it easier when it happens to you. Even in the best circumstances, financial hardship, pressure to find another employer, shattered confidence, and saying goodbye to friends, colleagues, and a familiar routine all contribute to the grief and stress of unemployment. But loss of livelihood can be made more manageable by learning to trust that you're competent and can skillfully navigate your difficulties, recognizing and accepting help from your resources, and understanding how to accept change with grace and wisdom.

Andre had a master's degree in statistics and successfully worked for many years as a "quant," performing quantitative analysis for large consulting firms like McKinsey and Moody's. After nearly two decades, his job felt routine and dull, but he liked the stability—no one called him on weekends and his commute was an easy fifteen-minute drive from his home. But that changed when his team was assigned to a new client—a small California hedge fund run by two partners, John and Derek. Both men were demanding and rude—if they didn't receive a response to an email within minutes, they called the team leader and complained, no matter what time or what day it was. Derek—though not a statistician—believed his experience as an investor and market analyst gave him enough expertise to challenge Andre and his colleagues, and when he told a junior quant named Tom—a young man that Andre mentored—on a conference call that Tom "didn't know what the fuck he was doing," Andre went to Kerri, the team leader and a vice president at the company. Kerri suggested the client was just an old crabby man who "wasn't that bad" and told Andre he should manage his group better because the project was generating a lot of revenue for their firm and she wouldn't want to be the one to jeopardize it.

That night, frustrated and angry, Andre talked to his wife about leaving, and a few weeks later, gave his notice. They took a two-week vacation in Rome, and when they got home, he talked to his recruiter, who set him up on a screening interview with Sylvia, the head of a consultancy that provided catalog data analysis to big retailers like J. Crew and Macy's. Andre knew he'd be a good fit, had plenty of experience, and no worries about the call, so he was surprised when Sylvia asked him specific questions about how to run highly technical software. He stammered and stumbled to respond and could hear her disappointment and annoyance with his ignorance, and when the call ended, he knew he'd blown it. His stomach sank and he felt himself panic as he texted his wife, "I shit the bed!" He was completely demoralized and afraid he'd been overconfident about his abilities and would never find another job.

If you're unexpectedly without work, do your best not to panic or sink into gloom. It's important to keep a clear head so you can make good decisions for yourself and the people who rely on you during this change. Be sure to pause, take a break, sit down, and breathe—at least five full inhalations and exhalations—before you speak or act.

The emotional stress from job hunting can be daunting and a blow to your self-esteem. Andre lost his confidence, bemoaned his decision to quit his stable position, and feared he would not find another suitable situation with the same or better salary and benefits. Like many people, his career provided him with a sense of purpose and value, and without one, he felt worthless and undeserving. He noticed how much his identity as an employee, a professional, and a breadwinner meant to him and how little he appreciated his other roles and qualities—as a husband, a friend, and an ethical, caring person. After talking with his therapist, Andre remembered that this identity had been built from the same roles and qualities that he now disdained and that he could use them to restore his confidence and to guide him through the hiring process. He shared his worries with his wife and felt buoyed by her appreciation for his kindness and good sense. He took a suggestion from his brother and enrolled in a software tutorial and ran practice data sets and projections. He felt more secure in his abilities during his next interview, which went well. Although he didn't get that job, he was convinced it was just a matter of time before he did, and a few months later he started working at an asset management firm.

For other people, losing a job is less about self-esteem or purpose and more a matter of survival. In such situations, the economic strain of unemployment can be a cause for profound anxiety and fear. Maria, a mother of two, worked twenty hours a week as a clerk for the local dry cleaner, while her husband worked at a popular French bistro as a back waiter. Their second baby was six months old when the COVID-19 pandemic began, and although afraid of catching the virus, Maria continued her job. But business was very slow—people weren't going to work or to celebratory events so there weren't dirty shirts to launder or cocktail dresses to clean. Soon, the store owners closed the shop from Sunday through Thursday and reduced Maria's hours to Saturday mornings from nine until noon. As a part-time worker, she wasn't eligible for unemployment benefits and nobody else was hiring. Then her husband's restaurant closed too. They had very little savings and weren't sure how they could pay for food, diapers, and everything else they needed. Maria's parents and brothers lived in Colombia, but she didn't want to ask them for help—they had their own struggles as the pandemic devastated their country too. For several months, the future looked bleak and hopeless, and Maria couldn't sleep, lost weight, and worried continually.

Worrying about finances is a leading cause of mental health problems, divorce, and even suicide, and wondering where and how your basic needs will be met is terrifying. Maria and her husband did their best not to blame each other or argue, but both were scared and ashamed they didn't have more opportunities and unsure who to ask or where to look for resources or assistance. Luckily, they were not alone—so many of their friends and neighbors were also out of work, and their church began an outreach program for parishioners in need. It offered a weekly food pantry, helped Maria apply for emergency assistance, and told her about the eviction moratorium—that their landlord could not evict them during the pandemic, even if they couldn't pay their rent. When their family started receiving a weekly federal unemployment stipend of $600 a week thanks to the CARES Act, it didn't go far, but they were no longer hungry and felt more secure about surviving until the crisis ended.

In difficult circumstances, it's useful to remember that you can count on the fact that everything changes—it's 100 percent guaranteed that you will never again be in the exact same situation you're in right now. You'll find the job you want, a different job, or maybe you won't find one for a long time and you'll have to move in with your friends. But by acknowledging the truth of change, you'll be more open to different possibilities, free to recognize opportunities when they arise, and better able to avoid disappointment when things don't go exactly the way you want. After more than a year of unemployment, Maria's husband unexpectedly got a job at American Airlines, and she's back at work at the dry cleaner. Their circumstances are better than they were before the pandemic began.

In the Buddhist tradition, no matter how helpless we might feel, we can always offer our aspirations—our best qualities—for ourselves and other people. Even if you're debilitated due to illness or injury, low on funds and without material goods, or depressed and sure you have nothing valuable to contribute, your wisdom, love, compassion, and kindness are priceless. Giving them away through aspiration is an easy way to regain your sense of worthiness and confidence and a reminder of the preciousness of your life.

Making aspirations are easy. Simply think of someone you know who is in need—your neighbor, your sister, someone you saw on the internet—and say: "May you benefit from my compassion and patience," "I give you my kindness to ease your pain," or "I wish you to be at peace"—whatever seems like an appropriate support. Making aspirations has an effect on our minds by helping to rewire our habitual patterns of fear, self-loathing, and despair into pathways of gratitude, gladness, and contentment. You don't have to believe in God or even that these aspirations have an effect on anyone outside of yourself for them to give you encouragement and hope.

Practice 14: Opening to Change

The version of *metta* (loving-kindness) meditation I offer here is traditionally used to develop equanimity—a sense of balance and ease in all circumstances—which can be particularly helpful during uncertain times, like when you're fired or unemployed. It's a wise reminder that no matter how hard we try or how much we want something, everything is always changing, impermanent, and unpredictable.

1. Find a quiet place, get still, take a few deep exhalations and inhalations, and put your hand on your heart.

2. Think of someone close to you who is struggling, upset, or in pain. Imagine that person with you and say to him or her silently: *May you be undisturbed by the changes in life.* Repeat this phrase slowly and intentionally while holding the wish that this person really hears you.

3. Next say to yourself silently: *May I be undisturbed by the changes in life.* Put your hand on your heart and repeat this sentence to yourself with as much caring and concern as you offered the other person.

4. You can share this wisdom by imagining all the people throughout the world who are struggling right now with unemployment, who are looking for work, or who have been fired as you say: *May we be undisturbed by the changes in life.*

5. Before you conclude this practice, take a few moments to sit silently, allowing yourself to breathe, maybe putting your hand on your heart or gently brushing your cheeks with your fingertip. Don't forget to say thank you to yourself for your efforts.

CHAPTER 15

Loss during a Crisis

To spare oneself from grief at all cost can be achieved only at the price of total detachment, which excludes the ability to experience happiness.

—ERICH FROMM[1]

NAVIGATING GRIEF IS HARD ENOUGH UNDER NORMAL CIRCUM-stances, but when a loss occurs against the backdrop of a larger crisis—like a pandemic, hurricane, or war—it can complicate the mourning process. When Frieda's "Hina Auntie"—her mother's eighty-year-old sister—died, Frieda struggled about whether to attend the funeral puja in person. It was during the height of the COVID-19 crisis before vaccines were available. Frieda felt she should go to the puja because her cousin Kati was suffering much more than she was—Kati had cared for her mom by herself at home during the pandemic, and she was now facing her death alone too, while Frieda was safe and sound, working from home in her light-filled Houston apartment. The ceremony was being held indoors in a small, enclosed space, and neither of Frieda's elderly parents nor her siblings planned to attend, but Frieda felt guilty and worried about Kati, who was grieving her mom while organizing a funeral and learning to adjust to living alone. Torn about what was the right thing to do, Frieda was relieved when her mom called and insisted that she not attend. She reminded her daughter that it was foolish to risk getting sick, which wouldn't help Kati or anyone else. "Better to appreciate that you're healthy and able to support Kati in other ways," she said, and Frieda agreed. She kept in close contact with her cousin via text and phone calls, joined her mom and other family members for the puja via Zoom, and perhaps most important, allowed herself to feel the heartbreak of watching Kati there with the priest, both wearing face masks and standing six feet apart, as they prayed over her aunt's body without other mourners.

During a crisis like a pandemic, natural disaster, economic depression, or civil unrest, a personal loss can feel insignificant or small in comparison with the struggles of others around you. You might think that getting fired isn't that big of a deal because at least you have a home and savings when so many others have lost their jobs and can't even pay for groceries or rent. Or maybe you think losing your home in a tornado is nothing compared to the death of a thirty-year-old father of two young kids whose appendix burst when the hospital lost power and his surgery was canceled. Although it's true that some losses are harder to recover from—some are tragic whereas others are difficult—it doesn't help us to compare our struggle to another's.

> During a time of collective struggle, remember it's okay to include yourself in your circle of compassion. Doing so in no way diminishes your capacity to support or love others who may be experiencing greater need or more difficult circumstances than you are. Put your hand on your heart and say: *May we all be safe and healthy.*

Comparison is a type of judgment that makes us believe we're either worse or better than someone else. In terms of suffering, we use comparison to decide who deserves our care and attention— giving more kindness, compassion, and love to those we feel need it more and offering less kindness, compassion, and love to those we feel need it less. But in the Buddhist tradition, qualities of love and compassion are indiscriminate. We don't pick and choose who gets our love—we offer it to everyone impartially, and that includes ourselves. Because love and compassion are immeasurable, we don't have to worry about not having enough, and we can share it with all, no matter their circumstances. With our actions, of course, we might distribute our compassion differently—giving more time, donations, or other resources to those most in need—but the wisdom of indiscriminate love acknowledges that all of our lives are precious, fragile, vulnerable, and interdependent. Indiscriminate love recognizes that those with easy happy lives, those who are dangerous, those who are devastated, like all of us, are suffering humans who want to be happy and not suffer and who will encounter loss, struggle, sickness, aging, and death.

Appreciation is a more skillful way than comparison to acknowledge the differences between us and others. Rather than pitying those who we think are worse off than we are or envying those who seem to have it better, we can simply appreciate what we have—no matter how little or how much it might be. During hard times, when we're all affected by troubles like the pandemic, a drought, or political instability, we can maintain a balanced and realistic view of both our difficulties and our blessings so we can meet everyone's struggles with wisdom, love, and compassion. Appreciation doesn't mean overlooking your needs or the injustices that exist in the world, but rather letting yourself be grateful for your resources so you can use them to support yourself and other people too.

From the Buddhist view, each one of us possesses inherent wholesome qualities—love, compassion, joy, and wisdom. Together they're called the *Brahmaviharas*—the Four Immeasurables—mind states that we can cultivate to alleviate our suffering and bring about beneficial actions for ourselves and others. It might seem like we or other people lack these qualities, but they're always present although sometimes obscured by our habits and conditioning as well as our confusion, neediness, greed, hatred, aversion, or ignorance.

Loving-kindness, which is the same as love or *metta*, is the wish for you and others to be happy; compassion or *karuna* is the wish for you and others to be free from suffering; joy or *mudita* is the delight we feel about the success and good fortune of others and ourselves; and wisdom or *upekkha* is the knowledge that although we can't control everything, our words and deeds matter because they have an effect on ourselves and each other. All of us can develop these beautiful qualities through meditation, skillful speech and behavior, and when we do, we'll become more loving, compassionate, joyful, and equanimous. In a crisis, we can rely on these gifts to prevent us from becoming trapped in greed or stupidity and instead allow them to guide us to the wisest and smartest actions for ourselves and our community.

Practice 15: Shared Suffering

During a crisis there is so much to worry about and so many people are in danger, vulnerable, or injured that it can seem like our loss is nothing special. We can feel like we're stuck all alone with our pain. But because we know there are countless people all over the world going through similar experiences to ours, who feel the same heartbreak, sadness, and loss, it's obvious that many others share our experience and feel the way we do.

Even if their loss is not exactly the same as ours, everyone is affected during a crisis, though perhaps not equally. For example, during the pandemic, three million people in the world lost their lives; many others lost their jobs. Marriages crumbled due to the stress of quarantine, and individuals of all ages and means watched with despair as plans, dreams, and friendships dissolved as a result of the closing of businesses and schools and the stress of social isolation.

If we allow ourselves to truly pay attention to global suffering, compassion naturally arises as we sense and acknowledge in our heart how difficult life is for everyone. The following meditation is based on a traditional Buddhist technique designed to help you awaken to the deep connection all living beings share and arouse your natural tenderness and care—for yourself and others.

1. Begin by finding a quiet place where you can be undisturbed. Sit, close your eyes or gaze softly at the ground, and put your hand on your heart. Take a few deep breaths.

2. Think of a loved one who is struggling. Imagine the person is here with you, and say: *May your struggles be eased. May you be at peace.* Continue silently, repeating the words again and again.

3. After five minutes or so, let go of this loved one, and make a connection with yourself. You might imagine you're looking in the mirror, gazing into your own eyes. Now give yourself the phrases: *May my struggles be eased. May I be at peace.*

4. Finally, consider all the other people on the earth right now who are experiencing your same loss. All the people grieving their mothers, who left their husbands, who got fired this very day—and give all of them the blessings from your heart: *May our struggles be eased. May we be at peace.*

CHAPTER 16

Unspoken Loss

Mourning is left behind, thanks to mourning itself.
—EMILE DURKHEIM[1]

IT WAS DECEMBER AND JACKIE HADN'T SEEN GINA SINCE AUGUST. They'd kept in touch by texting from time to time, mainly about the Steelers, their favorite hometown sports team—but little of real importance. They finally met up for pulled pork and short ribs. It was cold but pleasant as they sat on the crowded outdoor patio under the heat lamps drinking the local IPA on tap.

They'd been there nearly an hour, Jackie had finished her sandwich, and they'd both had two glasses of beer when Gina said, "I have to tell you something," and dissolved into tears. She told Jackie that her wife, Cheri, had miscarried in October. She was eleven weeks along and they were going to wait another week before they told anyone when Cheri started bleeding and cramping the day before Halloween. When they got to the hospital, they were told they'd lost the baby. Gina apologized for crying because she thought she really shouldn't be so upset—after all, *she* hadn't been pregnant, plus Cheri hadn't been very far along anyway—but she felt so disappointed and sad. "My mom keeps telling me to let it go—we can still have another baby, but I can't seem to get over it."

If you experience sadness for the death of someone that you don't know well or never met, or for someone who other people say isn't important enough for you to mourn, you're likely encountering disenfranchised grief. Try not to get defensive about your emotions or make others understand why you feel the way you do, but instead seek out a sympathetic person like an old friend, a spiritual guide, or a grief counselor.

Some passings—like a miscarriage—might feel less significant or too small to mourn compared to conventional tragedies or deaths. But all losses present significant reasons for mourning, and there is no loss so small that it cannot have an effect on us. Even when someone we dislike or haven't seen in a long time dies, we might feel sad or even abandoned by them. This happened to Sari. She'd been divorced from Mitchell for five years when she heard that he'd died. Although they'd fought nearly every day for the last four years of their twelve-year marriage, she felt like someone had kicked her to the floor after his sister Susan messaged her on Facebook and told her that he'd died a few months earlier of acute pancreatitis. Sari was happily remarried, and when she told her husband what happened, he shrugged and couldn't understand why it would matter so much to her. She felt stupid and sorry for grieving someone she hadn't seen or even cared much about for such a long time, and although it continued to disturb her, she didn't talk to anyone about it again.

Disenfranchised grief is the clinical term used to describe bereavement caused by a passing that isn't as accepted, common, or traditional compared to the expected occasions we have for bereavement. It can include acquaintances, friends you haven't seen in decades, patients or clients that you know strictly in a professional capacity, or relatives that you've never met. If you experience disenfranchised grief, you might feel you have to justify or defend your emotions or you may feel ashamed and hide them. You might sense you can't share your hurt with other people or that no one can understand what you're going through, leading you to grow angry and lonely.

Pablo was shocked when he opened the letter from a law firm that had helped his family buy a house in Arizona a decade earlier. It announced that the lawyer that represented him—Ron Copa—had died, and as his client, Pablo would need to request the files from his old case in writing, or the firm would destroy them in ninety days. Pablo had met Ron only a few times, but he was such a friendly person that he was hard to forget. They were both Catholic and Ron half-jokingly told Pablo that he converted to Catholicism when he got married and now was more devout than his wife, and that's why they had six children. He asked to see photos of Pablo's kids and was sincerely happy—he called to congratulate him—when their family moved into their house. Pablo wondered what happened to Ron—they were the same age—and he searched online and learned that he'd died quickly and unexpectedly from COVID-19. To Pablo it was senseless and upsetting, and when he called several friends to tell them about it, they said he was overreacting, which made him feel foolish.

We're all affected by each other in myriad ways, and sometimes our hearts are touched by a near-stranger, or we remember the long-ago potential of a young person now old, or we grieve the promise and possibilities that were unexpectedly lost. Although there are fewer resources available for this type of mourning—it's impossible to request bereavement leave, for example—it's still important to recognize how you feel and bring tenderness to your sadness. This includes the disenfranchised grief that arises when we mourn those who society says don't deserve it—murderers, rapists, or others who've performed acts of violence and great harm. But the people who've committed these terrible crimes have families too, and when they die, their parents or siblings might be crushed but unable to openly reveal their hurt. Their children might believe they have no right to mourn such an awful person, even if that awful person is their mom or dad.

Disenfranchised grief can become more complicated given the lack of support and being denied participation in normal rites like funerals and other services. You might feel angry that your feelings aren't validated or that you've been left alone with so much to manage on your own. Now is the time to become a good friend to yourself. Even if others can't hear you, *you* can hear you, so allow yourself to sit quietly, feel your emotions, and receive the space and time you need to heal.

In Buddhism, a root cause of our suffering is attachment or clinging. If we hold too tightly to an idea, a feeling, a desire, an opinion, a demand, anything at all—we will cause—or add to—pain. This includes our feelings. If you experience emotions that you don't want to have and you're attached to the idea that they should go away or you shouldn't have them, you'll likely feel even worse. The way to work with any of our thoughts or beliefs or sentiments is to just *allow* them. *Allowing* means you don't have to add to them, make them go away, or even figure them out. You can just sit with them—with kindness and patience—and allow them to just be. Another term for allowing is to *let go*—let go of trying to push emotions away or change them at all. Without attachment to feeling a certain way, your disenfranchised grief can be heard and understood by you as you let yourself move through the grieving process.

Practice 16: Welcoming Peace

If you're feeling alone or abandoned in your grieving process and perhaps believe that others can't or won't validate your experience, you can always offer yourself peace and love to soothe and regulate your body and mind.

1. Find a tranquil spot where you can rest undisturbed. This could be a quiet corner of your kitchen or living room, a seat in your backyard, or a bench in a nearby park.

2. Shut off your devices and take a few deep inhalations and exhalations. Let your belly expand when you breathe in, and contract when you breathe out.

3. Bring your attention to your body. Notice the weight of your body on your seat, feel your clothing touching your skin, allow the sounds to enter your ears.

4. Close your eyes and imagine yourself. You might picture yourself as you look in the mirror, or you might envision your child self.

5. Smile and send a few relaxing breaths to yourself.

6. Put your hand on your heart and say: *I welcome everything that is in my heart. May I sense the peace that is always within me.* Repeat these words to yourself for a few moments.

7. Include others in your visualization—everyone dear to you—your closest family, friends, and pets, and say: *May we welcome everything that is in our heart. May we sense the peace that is*

always within us. Repeat for a few minutes, then include everyone in the world and repeat for a moment more.

8. Conclude by thanking yourself for your willingness to let love and peace into your heart and to heal.

CHAPTER 17

When It's Time to Say Goodbye

Heartbreak may be the very essence of being human, of being on the journey from here to there, and of coming to care deeply for what we find along the way.

—DAVID WHYTE[1]

I WAS IN CHICAGO, SITTING AT DENISE'S BEDSIDE WHILE SHE WAS dying. I rubbed her feet and recited silent prayers. She was bloated and emaciated from metastasized liver cancer, and I hardly recognized her. She was no longer responsive—eyes closed, breathing through her mouth, her limbs heavy at her sides—and it was clear she had only a short time left to live. Lori had called me five days before and told me I should come and say goodbye, and although I could have been there sooner, I dreaded this terrible, final visit and put it off for as long as possible.

Just a month earlier, after we'd learned she was out of treatment options, Denise, Lori, and I sat together around her dining room table with the hospice nurse, asking questions that now seemed ridiculous: Could she do chair yoga? Would eating all organic food improve and extend her life? At that time, we could see she was growing weaker and slower and spending more time in bed. She was less and less engaged with other people and the world—disinterested in books, movies, and conversations that had been so important to her—but in my mind that didn't necessarily mean she was going to *die*. I thought maybe the doctors could adjust her medications and she'd have less pain and more energy—diminished and limited but alive. I knew the cancer would continue to spread and that it would inevitably kill her, but I didn't think it would be so soon. It wasn't exactly that I was in denial, but more that I'd known her for so long and loved her so much that I truly could not conceive of a time when she would no longer exist.

> Sometimes an ending has a quality of unreality. You might think, "Is this really happening?" or feel detached or disconnected from your body and your heart. If this happens to you when you're saying goodbye, take a few deep breaths. Then rub your hands together—palm to palm—briskly for thirty seconds to one minute, and place one hand on your heart and the other on your belly and take a few gentle and full breaths.

The day was bright and hot but the room was still and pleasant, the windows closed against the heat. Denise's breathing was labored but steady, and occasionally she groaned—from pain or worry or perhaps dreams. Her sister carefully and kindly attended to her needs, giving her medications, wiping her face, repositioning her frail body, adjusting the sheets to make her as comfortable as possible. The hospice nurses came and left several times, and as the day waned, other loved ones joined us at Denise's bedside. For a time, her friend Laura sat on her right, with Brant on her left, holding her hand and tenderly whispering reassurances to her. Lori and I sat next to each other at the bedside, she quietly whispering to Denise and sharing how much she loved her while I stroked our friend's arms and legs, telling her she was safe and didn't need to be afraid.

Helplessly watching my dear friend's life fade as the hours passed, I felt more and more anguish, and when I stood up to turn on the table lamp in the now-dark room, I noticed a terrible heaviness in my chest as if my heart weighed one hundred pounds. I felt like I could sink right through the floor into the earth and even wished it would happen because I really didn't think I could bear losing Denise. As I took a deep breath, my hand on my belly, I heard a voice in my mind gently say, "Love is stronger than death." That's when I suddenly understood—with terrible sadness and relief—that dying would make no difference in the way I felt about Denise. My love for her wouldn't disappear—it would continue for as long as I was alive. When she died later that night, I knew it was okay to say goodbye because she would always be my beloved friend, even if she was no longer with me, and I was grateful I could be there with her until the end.

Seeing a friend for the last time, leaving an office where you've worked for years, moving out of your family home—very few moments are as hard as saying goodbye. It requires fortitude and courage to face these losses and deep wisdom to accept painful or undesired changes, but with patience, mindfulness, and kindness to ourselves, we can show up for these moments without ignoring or denying any of our human experiences.

Some of us, like my father, for example, are unable to tolerate an ending. When his favorite uncle, Red, moved from Chicago to Las Vegas, Dad skipped the goodbye party. Although Red called him several times before he left, my father refused to talk to him and only resumed communications months after Red had relocated. After Dad and my mother divorced, they sold the family home, and on the day of the closing he came to the house and shouted at the movers and my mom that they were a bunch of assholes who didn't know what the hell they were doing. Even though the divorce had been his idea and he already lived in another house with another woman, saying good-bye to his former life and home was too painful and scary to bear, so the only way he knew to react was with fear, anger, and blame.

In *Tao Te Ching*, an ancient Chinese philosophical text, it's said that in each of our human lives, we'll experience both ten thousand joys *and* ten thousand sorrows. It's important to notice that the author, Laozi, used the conjunction *and* not *but*—to let us know we must include everything that happens, good or bad, like it or not. We do this because avoiding an ending or insisting that the inescapable is escapable only causes us more suffering and pain because it's the reality of our poignant human condition. In other spiritual traditions, opening to the truth of life is called a state of grace—a quality of acceptance that includes gratitude and surrendering to the mystery of existence and the natural order of things. This state of grace can be cultivated, so that when we face an ending—tragic or not—we can offer ourselves and others our full presence and compassion without running away or trying to deny what's happening.

In the Buddhist tradition, we can create a state of grace by practicing generosity, patience, and love. We can offer our words and actions to support everyone involved to avoid creating hard feelings or causing more upset in an often already difficult situation. We can give patience to our fears, agitation, sorrow, or anger, and do the same for others. And we can share our love with everyone who is saying goodbye, including ourselves, with appreciation for all of our joys and sorrows too.

In early teachings, the Buddha's compassion was described as a "great brave heart." That's because compassion—the quality of not turning away from suffering and actually moving toward it to help alleviate it—requires unfathomable courage. Facing suffering—in ourselves or in others—can be terribly scary, and most of us want to get as far away from it as we can.

The courage of compassion is like that of a firefighter, parent, or doctor. It arises from a deep sympathy with anyone suffering, with a fierce determination to dispel misery in whatever way is possible,* even if it's risky or frightening. This kind of compassion is free from pity because it recognizes that suffering is universal and no one is immune to it. It's also free from despair, because a great brave heart understands that everything—even suffering—is impermanent and inevitably ends.

Practice 17: Grace

You don't have to believe in God to surrender to the tender and beautiful moments of life and to allow yourself to be held by the presence and mystery of being human. Accepting that you're powerless over the comings and goings of events is a type of faith in something bigger than yourself—maybe God, nature, or science—and this faith can help you stop battling against forces beyond your control so you can rest, appreciate, and trust in the ordinary order of the world in which we live.

1. Find a quiet spot where you won't be disturbed.

2. Bring your attention to your breath, breathe deeply, and put your hand on your heart or your belly, where you can feel your inhalations and exhalations. Notice what is happening—scary thoughts, shallow breathing, tightness in your chest. Whatever it is, silently say "yes" to it as you welcome it like a troubled friend or a crying child.

3. Imagine you're in touch with a powerful, gentle, and steady force. This might be the Judeo-Christian-Islamic God, deities from the Buddhist, Hindu, or other traditions, or what recovery groups call a "higher power" or the universe. I often connect with the mystery of life and death and this common presence or spark that joins all living beings.

4. Put your hand on your heart and feel your feet on the ground. When you exhale, rest into this powerful force with a sigh of letting go—of your ideas, plans, and strategies. Let your shoulders drop and relax your jaw and other places that might be tense.

5. Now, give up and let go of your wants, your dread, your terror, to this powerful force. Say silently, "I surrender to that which I cannot control," or "I surrender to life as it is," or any other words or actions, like taking a deep breath and exhaling or holding your palms face up that help you release your struggle.

6. To end this practice, take a moment to rest with your breath, and then thank yourself and your powerful force.

CHAPTER 18

When People Behave Badly

Let go of the battle. Breathe quietly and let it be. Let your body relax and your heart soften. Open to whatever you experience without fighting.

—JACK KORNFIELD[1]

WE EXPECT OUR FAMILIES AND FRIENDS TO COME TOGETHER during difficult times and read and hear lots of pretty stories about siblings who set aside differences to care for an aging parent, divorced spouses who hold each other up after the death of a child, and large blended families cheerfully sharing their resources after a tornado destroys a cousin's farm. Sadly, these stories are the exception, not the rule. The stress, fear, and confusion that arises during times of great loss doesn't always bring out the best in people, and many times will, in fact, bring out their worst, like being unable to manage difficult emotions and unwilling to trust or cooperate with others. In fact, I've personally heard and experienced many more difficult situations—in which someone behaved badly—than those where all went well. Several people close to me are still reeling from the devastation caused by the poor behavior of friends and family members during or after a crisis or death.

Britney was long divorced with a grown daughter, Teri, with whom she trusted and shared a close and loving relationship, despite living in different cities. When Britney got sick, she appointed Teri as her healthcare proxy, but after her diagnosis was changed to terminal, only two months before she died, Britney abruptly changed the proxy to her childhood friend, Hope. She told everyone that it was because Teri lived so far away, but it didn't make sense to anyone because Teri was always happy and able to travel to visit her mom and had already been to stay and help care for Britney several times during her long illness.

Britney's family and friends were concerned about her choice because Hope was a divisive person. She was controlling, gossipy, and quick to find fault with others. She was also exploitative, charging Britney for gas when she drove her to treatment or picked up her groceries, which offended those closest to Britney who wouldn't dream of accepting payment from their dear sick friend. Also, Hope was strangely possessive of her relationship with Britney, insisted on talking with her doctors privately, and on the days when it was her turn to care for her friend, made it clear that others were unwelcome in Britney's home—although Britney had told them she wanted and needed her loving support network with her as often as possible.

Sadly, it's not uncommon for dying people to be manipulated into making changes to their will or healthcare directives. Like so many in that position, Britney was vulnerable, afraid of the pain and suffering of cancer and of how her illness and death would affect the people she loved the most. She wanted to believe Hope when she said that she would ensure her a painless death and would be more able to handle the grief than others. Of course, neither promise was possible or true.

If you're dealing with a difficult person during a death or crisis and you're losing your patience, take a time-out. Go to another room, sit in your car, or leave the situation for a while by going for a walk or a drive to calm your nervous system, clear your head, and refresh your being. Put your hand on your heart and say to yourself silently, "May I be patient with all that's in my heart."

When Britney was on her deathbed, unconscious with only hours to live, Hope predictably grew increasingly difficult and controlling. Profound loss can be so destabilizing that troubled people become even more troubled, and Hope was no exception. As friends and family peacefully sat at Britney's bedside, reassuring her and holding her hand, Hope randomly asked one to leave because she'd been there too long, lied to another when the person called and told them they weren't welcome to see Britney, and texted someone else that she could not come to say goodbye to her old friend. Teri and Britney's closest friends felt helpless to intervene and when, at midnight, Hope announced that Britney was being moved to a facility for better care and pain management, they were shocked. The hospice nurse had already advised against this, and any sane person could see that Britney shouldn't be disturbed or moved from her home—she was as comfortable as a dying person could be, her cat was at her side, and her pain medication was administered regularly. The ambulance came and the emergency medical technicians wheeled Britney—fragile and helpless—out of her home on a gurney while her poor cat cried and her family wept. Teri insisted she ride with her mother on the way to hospice, because Britney unsurprisingly died in the ambulance only minutes after leaving her home. Those who loved Britney were heartbroken that her peaceful passing was so violently and ill-advisedly disrupted.

Death and dying, job loss, and divorce are so disturbing that even the best of us may struggle to keep our patience, manage our anger, and avoid freaking out and panicking from sheer terror. These terrible losses trigger other past losses, and old wounds resurface, making it hard to discern how or if the past is affecting the present. So it's unreasonable to expect that your alcoholic sister-in-law or your frequently enraged son—individuals who struggle with common day-to-day pressures—will be able to handle the stress and confusion of a profound loss with calm, concern for others, cooperation, or kindness. It simply may not be possible for them.

My mom made many bad decisions in her life, and chief among them were many of her friendships. She was attracted to liars, drinkers, and cruelty and had many times been swindled or taken advantage of—she lent Jamie from the Chatterbox $4,000 and he moved to Green Bay and never paid it back; she loaned her car to Kristina, who totaled it when she ran into a Wausau Paper truck coming out of the mill; and thanks to a phone solicitor, she put her meager savings into an annuity, where she was unable to access it when she needed it the most. When she was dying in the hospital hospice ward, I returned from lunch one day to find two middle-aged women I didn't know sitting at her bedside, surprised to see me. After I introduced myself, Sheila and Pat asked, "What are you doing here?" Feeling a bit confused at such a strange question, I explained that I was there to take care of my mom. They quickly left, but soon after, Lori noticed that the cross my mom had been wearing around her neck and her garnet ring were missing. Neither piece of jewelry was important to me or valuable, and I hesitated to accuse anyone of stealing or to make a fuss about it—I just wanted to ignore it, considering it perhaps the final example of my mom's bad judgment. But Lori—bravely indignant on my mom's behalf—made some phone calls and tracked down these women, and on the day of my mom's memorial service, Pat came to the funeral home and returned them to us.

When other people behave badly, what's most important is to make sure *you* don't behave badly. You might feel like telling your brother he's an unreliable jerk who never contributed to your family, but even if that's true, it's not the time to say it. We can endure difficult people with wisdom and equanimity, knowing we can't change them but doing our best to prevent them from harming us or our loved ones, without showing them hatred or ill will. You might have to ask your brother to leave the hospital when your dad is dying or tell your aunt she can't remove things from your recently passed mom's home without permission. But you can do it with patience and calm, remembering that how *they* act isn't up to us, but how *we* act, is.

For a long time after Britney's death, her two oldest and closest friends, Kate and Lee, struggled with anger over Hope's behavior. They felt that what she'd done was unforgivable and secretly wished she'd be punished or condemned for her bad behavior. After a few months of being torn up inside with outrage and grief, Kate's husband told her she had to let it go—*Hope* wasn't being harmed by her outrage—*Kate* was. Kate decided he was right, and she needed to find a way to forgive—not for Hope, but for herself.

In the Buddhist tradition, forgiveness is a practice of letting go of your own hatred, hostility, and anger over a harm or hurt that's been done in the past. You do it to free yourself from afflicting emotions that disturb your mind—you don't do it to absolve the person that caused the harm. Forgiveness is a choice to heal yourself by letting go of poisonous emotions that are causing you pain, and it doesn't mean condoning or justifying bad behavior nor does it mean that you have to have contact with the person who caused the injury. It just means you've decided not to hang on to your suffering in order to process your grief, let go of the past, and look forward to the future with openness, relief, and love.

As a Buddhist student, I've chosen to take certain vows that support my intention to develop wisdom and compassion for all beings. These include the Five Precepts and also the bodhisattva vows. The Five Precepts involve discipline and restraint and are a promise not to kill, steal, sexually harm, deceive, or abuse intoxicants. If you take the Five Precepts and break one of these promises—for example, telling your boss you were late because of traffic when you actually overslept—then you broke the vow not to deceive, and you need to take it again. (Which is why many Buddhists recite the precepts daily, both to remind themselves of their vows and to amend for those that they've broken.)

On the other hand, the bodhisattva vow—a commitment to become a bodhisattva to benefit all beings—is *unbreakable*. There's nothing you can do that will void or damage it—if you make a mistake or do something unskillfully, it's okay, your intention is still intact. But there is one big exception—if you completely and utterly give up on someone, you've broken the bodhisattva vow. So if you believe something like, "I hate this person so much that even if she was hit by a car in front of me, I wouldn't lift a finger to help" or "This person deserves to be abused because he has done so many mean things," you've broken the bodhisattva vow because *bodhisattvas never give up on anyone*. They know that all humans are struggling and suffering, including those who are dangerous or harmful. A bodhisattva might use her wisdom to make sure a murderer goes to prison where he can't hurt anyone again but would not hate the murderer or wish him ill. Bodhisattvas use their compassion to continue to wish the murderer peace of mind and the conditions to be without pain or suffering so as to be free of the causes that led him to act with violence or hatred.

Practice 18: Forgive and Remember

There is a misconception that forgiveness means pretending or forgetting that an injury or harmful act ever happened. That's not the case—real forgiveness is a wise act that encourages us to remember the bad that happened so that we can learn from it and prevent it from happening again to ourselves or others. It can also seem like forgiveness means letting someone get away with something—that it enables them to avoid punishment or facing the consequences of their poor or malicious behavior, but forgiveness doesn't mean we agree with what happened or that a wrong is actually a right, and it doesn't mean that we wouldn't seek redress, make a complaint, or even contact the authorities if necessary. Forgiveness simply means that we no longer cling to the hatred, anger, enmity, cruelty, or ill will that we may harbor inside us so that we can be liberated from the pain and struggle of such mind states.

Forgiveness is a process—it's not possible to snap your fingers and suddenly feel okay about past injury—but the following contemplation is a good way to begin. Please note that you might not want to forgive someone, and that's okay—you don't have to—it's not something you *should* do nor does it mean you're a better person for doing so. Or you might wish that you wanted to forgive and you're just not ready—and that's okay too. You can use the following practice however you like to bring compassion and relief to yourself and no one else.

1. Find a quiet and comfortable place where you won't be disturbed. You can lie down, sit, or walk—whatever feels most kind and easy for you. Put your hand on your belly and notice your breath. Keep breathing.

Begin your forgiveness practice by remembering moments when you've hurt others. Start with small harms, like when you got so mad at your mother that you hung up the phone on her or when you were rude to the clerk at the pharmacy after your order was lost. You might visualize these moments and feel the pain that you caused and also the regret of doing so. Realize that you acted from ignorance, confusion, or pain. Then silently say, "For any harm or suffering I've caused, please forgive me." Continue repeating this phrase for ten minutes or so.

2. Consider the many ways you've hurt yourself. You might recall self-criticism and judgment or situations when you abandoned yourself or abused your body or mind. Realize that you acted from ignorance, confusion, or pain. Remembering these thoughts, words, and actions that you've used to harm yourself and the anguish that you caused yourself, say to yourself silently, "For any harm or suffering I've caused myself, I forgive myself." Continue repeating this phrase for ten minutes or so.

3. Finally, remember moments when others have hurt you. You can visualize the many ways you've been wounded, injured, shamed, and harmed and tenderly recall how you felt—the sadness, anger, disgrace, fear, embarrassment. Realize that those who caused your suffering did so from ignorance, confusion, or pain, just as you have. Say silently to them: *To the extent that I am ready, for any harm or suffering that has happened to me, I offer my forgiveness.*

4. Before you conclude this meditation, take some time to let yourself be quiet and still. You can put your hand on your belly or your heart or gently stroke your face before you resume your regular activities.

CHAPTER 19

Don't Be Afraid to Laugh

Discovering more joy does not, I'm sorry to say, save us from the inevitability of hardship and heartbreak. In fact, we may cry more easily, but we will laugh more easily, too. We have hardship without becoming hard. We have heartbreak without being broken.
—ARCHBISHOP DESMOND TUTU[1]

Obe's father had a two-seat barbershop in River Grove for nearly forty years. Because the town was once known for the Mafia families that were said to live there during the seventies, his family nicknamed him the *barbliere*—a joking reference to the consigliere of the *Godfather* movies—although he wasn't Italian. When Obe's father died at age eighty-six, he'd been retired for decades, so Obe was surprised by how many of his dad's former clients came to the funeral home for the visitation. Many were his father's age, and they sat together in the lobby, drinking coffee and eating the crumb cake his sister Tooty baked. They were loud—old, hard of hearing, and so excited to be together that they were nearly shouting—and family and friends inside the viewing room could hear nearly everything they said.

Obe sat with Tooty and his mother, Gracie, right up front near the casket. His dad looked the same as he had last week—maybe better, Obe thought, thanks to the funeral director. He was wearing his best and only suit with his Masonic lapel pin, his hands folded peacefully across his chest. But as the old men's stories floated through the room, he could tell Tooty was getting more and more angry. "Aggravated," she called it—and he held her hand, wishing her not to upset their mother by exploding with rude words in frustration.

Then they heard the loudest of the men say, "There were always two in the seats and two waiting for a cut and two shooting the shit. I kid you not, sometimes I just went down there to hear the old man tell a story while he worked. Boy oh boy, could he tell a story! Like the one when he took Gracie to Atlantic City, and he won so much money he bought her a fox coat and one of those Rolex watches but then he lost so much she had to return them." The laughter was louder now and Obe froze—did his dad really lose money in Atlantic City? He didn't even know he gambled. He felt his sister sit up straight, her nostrils flaring, and he knew she was offended and about to stand up, march into the hallway, and tell everyone to leave. But then his mother joined the men's laughter, first a chuckle and then a full giggle, affirming the truth of the story and her love for the fun she had with her husband, which made Obe and Tooty laugh too, happy to know their dad was remembered, and free to express their relief that his life could still bring them all joy.

Death, dying, sickness, divorce, getting fired—these are all serious matters, and few of us would consider them a time for levity or fun. But even in the most terrible moments, when you're feeling despair, heartache, frustration, or fear, you can make room for joy and laughter, using lightheartedness and humor to skillfully discharge pent-up energy, distress, or frustration. Allowing for happiness in the face of hardship creates a balanced view of the situation—that no matter how dire, we can have gratitude and appreciation for ourselves and each other, and we don't have to cling too tightly to painful emotions—we can make room to hold both our sorrows and our joys equally.

You might notice you're feeling impatient, annoyed, or angry at the people around you if they aren't taking the situation as seriously as you think they should or at yourself for enjoying a silly moment with your family. It's okay. Enjoyment and pleasure can be held in equal measures with sadness and grief, without one diminishing or negating the other. When you hear laughter—yours or another's—silently say to yourself, "May our happiness increase."

After Britney died, Teri felt too guilty to enjoy herself since her mom could no longer do the same. Whenever someone suggested she watch a funny movie or get a pedicure, she refused, annoyed—her mother was dead after a long and painful illness, for god's sake, how could she enjoy herself? She believed that if she really loved her mother, she would not take a break from thinking about her and missing her for even one second. If she did, that would mean she was a bad person and an even worse daughter.

Many grieving people feel like this—that they must sacrifice their pleasure and happiness because the deceased can't share in it anymore. Whenever Lori and I see each other, we feel our dear friend Denise's absence powerfully, because for so many years the three of us were always together. At first it was too hard to be together because it was too painful without her and it felt so unfair that she wasn't there. But over time, we've realized that although Denise is no longer alive, she's always with us. When Lori and I are together now, we're able to enjoy each other and appreciate our friendship. We talk about our dear friend and remember how much fun we had when she choreographed a synchronized swimming dance and taught it to us in the pool at the Bellagio Hotel, and how much we laughed when she did a spot-on imitation of Kristen Wiig on the airplane in *Bridesmaids*. Now one of us will read a new book or go to a show and say happily, "Denise would've loved that." Our gladness and joy for friendship and each other *includes* our sadness at her passing—it doesn't negate it. As grief is less acute, what remains isn't the absence of sorrow, but rather the poignant truth that we still love her although she will not be able to share in our happiness again.

Sometimes people cling to their distress to signal to others that they're upset. A few weeks after Miguel lost his job of nearly ten years as a project manager following a restructuring in his office, his roommate invited him to join a running club followed by hamburgers at a local restaurant. Miguel felt that his friend wasn't recognizing how distressed he was about being fired and curtly refused. But his roommate didn't know and *couldn't*—unless Miguel told him.

Instead of indirectly trying to show people how upset you are, it's more skillful to share your upset, whatever it might be at that moment—anger, fear, annoyance, sadness, loneliness—with those close to you, while at the same time finding pleasure in your everyday activities and letting yourself heal. Clinging to a loss can easily develop into self-pity, a lonely mind state that suggests our suffering is less deserved or more powerful than that of other people. Self-pity lacks wisdom and disconnects us from the reality of the world, which is that everyone, without exception, encounters difficult changes.

When we live in harmony with this reality, we know our struggles are normal and shared, and we can offer our compassion and joy to everyone in this uncertain, tender, and brief human life.

Mudita, or appreciative joy, is the state of mind that arises when we delight or celebrate the success of others. It's the way you might feel when you're a guest at a wedding, sharing the happiness of the marrying couple, toasting to their love and joy. Or when you attend a graduation, sharing in the happy achievements of the students, feeling pleased and appreciative for them and their hard work.

Mudita is an opportunity to gladden our mind—to let go of anxious or distressing emotions—by connecting with the beauty and wonderfulness happening all around us all the time. His Holiness the Dalai Lama says that if we practice *mudita* we have endless occasions to be cheerful, simply by paying attention to and sharing the countless treasures we encounter every day—the birth of a baby, a modern new replacement for an old wheelchair, a successful surgery, an abandoned dog adopted, hard work rewarded, a promotion, a recovery from addiction, a healthy harvest—reminding us that our lives are interdependent not only in our shared suffering, but in our shared joy too.

Practice 19: Finding Joy

If you're unable to allow yourself to feel pleasure, happiness, or success because of a recent loss, it can be helpful to learn *mudita*, appreciative joy. *Mudita* is a mind state like compassion, love, and wisdom, which can be developed by paying attention with mindfulness and meditation practice. You can try the method here, and you can also keep a *mudita* journal by writing down at least one thing every day that made you feel joyful for another's happiness. That could include a singer who won a Grammy award, your brother's best friend who could finally afford a new used car, or your neighbor who's super happy for a visit with her grandchildren.

1. Shut off your devices. Find a quiet spot, get still, stop talking, and put your hand on your heart. Take a few breaths.

2. Imagine someone you know who's had a recent success, like a new job, a baby, or recovered from illness. Visualize the person sitting next to you, looking in your eyes. Repeat silently, *May your joy never cease.* Continue for five or more minutes.

3. After a few minutes, imagine a time when you've had an occasion for joy, like your wedding, when you got your first job, or when you passed a test. Imagine that you're looking in your own eyes in a mirror, and repeat silently, *May my joy never cease.* Continue for five or more minutes.

4. Now imagine the person you know, yourself, and everyone who's had success recently. You can think of all the celebrations that are happening all around the world for birthdays, graduations, good harvests, rebuilt homes, and restored health, and repeat silently for all of us, *May our joy never cease.*

5. Before you conclude this meditation, take a moment to acknowledge your efforts and say thank you to yourself.

CHAPTER 20

Caring for Dying People

Before you know kindness as the deepest thing inside,
you must know sorrow as the other deepest thing.
—NAOMI SHIHAB NYE[1]

ELIZABETH WAS A WEEK FROM HER ONE HUNDREDTH BIRTHDAY the last time I saw her. She was frail and in a wheelchair, but when her daughter Issa settled her at the dinner table, she was almost as engaged and alert as she'd ever been. She wore a thick, pale purple sweater that complemented her white, neatly combed hair, and when I told her she looked pretty, she said, "Not bad for nearly one hundred." She smiled and told us one hundred was too old and she hoped she'd die before then, but she didn't. She lived for another six months, and for most of that time, she was cared for by Issa with the help of other family members.

Issa, recently single, had bought a new condo but still hadn't moved into it. Instead, she lived out of bags and suitcases in her mom's spare bedroom, where she stayed most nights. She didn't plan it that way but it was clear her mother could no longer be alone. Elizabeth wasn't strong enough to walk without support, and she'd already fallen twice trying to get out of bed. The nursing care provided by hospice and Medicare came only a few hours a week, so during the day, a paid home attendant helped out when Issa and her brother were unable to be there. But after work, on nights and weekends, for nearly a year, Issa was the primary caregiver. She knew she didn't have to do it—it was her choice—but she still felt exhausted, frustrated, and sad.

> Don't forget to breathe. Caregivers can become so absorbed with their responsibilities that they might be breathing shallowly, too fast, or even holding their breath. As you inhale, let your belly expand, and as you exhale, let your belly contract.

Elizabeth was often confused and sometimes resented being sick and old. Some days she was lucid and alert, but other times she wasn't sure what day or year it was and wondered when her long-dead husband would get home from work. One night she told Issa that a cab had just dropped her off and insisted that Issa go outside and pay the driver. Issa said "Okay," but when she didn't get up and leave the room, Elizabeth angrily demanded that she hurry downstairs to the waiting driver. When Issa, exasperated, said, "Mom, you weren't in a taxi!" Elizabeth replied stubbornly, "Then how do you think I got home?" Issa could laugh at times like this, but other times her mom was demanding and resentful, telling her to stop bossing her around or that Issa didn't know what she was doing and that her nurse Sheila was a lot better at helping her than her own daughter.

Taking care of someone you love while they're sick or dying is among the most stressful situations you'll ever encounter. Unpaid caregivers are most often family members who report high rates of exhaustion and depression and often feel alone, disheartened, and overwhelmed. An elderly relative's lingering death can mean months of waiting for your life to return to normal, while simultaneously feeling guilt for thinking this, wishing for your loved one's well-being and happiness, and bracing yourself for the pain of their death and your loss.

Often, caregivers are expected to set aside their own needs—losing sleep, ignoring physical aches or pains, even sacrificing their own family or livelihood—because the needs of the dying person are so great. This pressure placed on caregivers is pervasive in our society, even among the caregivers themselves. In my neighbor Dan's case, he didn't want to spend a single evening or weekend away from his beloved wife Pam, fearing she would be upset or lonely without him. Even while she received hospice care at home, Dan insisted on cooking dinner and sharing it with her at her bedside. During the last few months of her life, Pam was taking morphine for pain and had little appetite, and friends recommended he take a break and invited him to eat dinner at their homes or offered to do the cooking for him. Although he yearned for companionship and conversation, he felt too guilty to accept it and said, "No thank you. I'll be fine. She's so sick I don't want to do anything that might upset her."

As they neglect their physical and social needs, caregivers often do the same with their feelings. Caring for a relative brings up so many past associations and triggers, but people feel encouraged to ignore them or shrug them off. Issa was surprised that despite being bedridden and helpless, Elizabeth still managed to hurt Issa's feelings and make her feel inadequate and small, just as she did in childhood. When she told Issa yet again that she trusted her brother Will more than Issa—"because you know I think men are more capable"—Issa felt tears welling up and left the room to cry in the bathroom. Although Will tried to dismiss it—"You know she didn't know what she was saying"—Issa knew better because Elizabeth had said it so many times in the past. She was especially hurt because *she* was the one who was there most of the time, not Will. All these old feelings—guilt, shame, anger, disappointment—are normal, yet caregivers often believe they shouldn't have them, mainly because of the seriousness of the situation. They believe that they should somehow "rise above it"—becoming saintlike and putting all their own needs aside, like their idea of an idealized good child, spouse, or grandchild.

Caregivers often feel that *all* of their energy must be given to their family member and that it's shameful to keep any for themselves. Self-care—mental, physical, and emotional—is not a selfish act. Pushing yourself beyond your physical and emotional capacity results in burnout and compassion fatigue, and it isn't noble or wise and it doesn't help anyone. Caregiver burnout can cause harm or even incapacitate, causing physical pain, injury, or mental illness like depression or debilitating anxiety. A truly loving person includes everyone in their heart, and your circle of care must contain *you*.

Shantideva, a great Indian Buddhist teacher from the first century, wrote *The Guide to the Bodhisattva's Way of Life*, which is a guidebook of wise and compassionate advice for spiritual seekers. In it he suggests that real wisdom means that before trying to give so much to others, we should first learn to "equalize self and other." Equalizing self and other means that no one is more deserving of love and happiness than you, and you're no more deserving of love and happiness than anyone else. In this way, we neither neglect our own suffering nor put our suffering above that of others. Instead, we understand that caring for ourselves is an expression of our deepest wisdom and strength and it enables us to meet difficult circumstances with a clear mind free of resentment, fear, and denial.

> Many people are attracted to spiritual practice because they want to be better people or to help others, and I was drawn to Buddhism for those reasons too—because I wanted to know how to help make a more equitable world and be a kinder person. One of my first teachers was a Tibetan nun, Venerable Robina Courtin, who is direct and no-nonsense, unafraid to challenge her students or show impatience when she thinks they're being deliberately obtuse or refusing to understand. So I was surprised when she gently responded to an earnest question from a young man with a soul patch wearing a Médecins Sans Frontières tee shirt who wanted to know how he

could help fix all the problems in the world. She said, "Petal,"—a term of endearment she often uses—"first you have to deeply understand your own suffering. Get really close to yourself and let your heart break for all you've been through and taste the vomit of your own confusion and pain. And then your compassion will be so great it will arise for you and for everyone else."

Caregiving can be a real opportunity to experience this profound realization—for yourself, your loved one, your family, and for the benefit of all beings.

Practice 20: Mindful Caregiving

Caring for a dying person takes such an emotional and physical toll on us and so much time that it might seem impossible or impractical to take a moment for yourself. The following practice makes it easier for you to rest by encouraging you to take frequent small breaks—five- to ten-minute moments.

1. Set a timer on your phone or your clock to ring every hour during the day or when you're awake.

2. When the alarm sounds, set a timer for five minutes. Then—*important!*—set aside your phone, computer, and other devices.

3. Stand up, stretch your hands above your head, and do a few gentle neck rolls as you take eight deep inhalations and exhalations.

4. You can sit or continue standing. Get still, close your eyes, put your hands on your belly and your heart, and take a few more deep inhalations and exhalations.

5. Bring your attention to the center of your chest where your ribcage rises and falls with your breath. See if you can keep your attention here, gently feeling your lungs expand and sensing when they relax.

6. Thoughts might arise for you, and when you notice you're thinking about something—a story, a worry, a plan—choose to let go of it and gather your awareness to your heart center.

7. Before you conclude the practice, say thank you for taking care of yourself and others. Repeat often.

CHAPTER 21

When You're Filled with Guilt or Regret

Look at all the things we become attached to, whether they are people or possessions or feelings or conditions of the body. Nothing we have, no one in our lives, no state of mind is exempt from change. Nothing at all can prevent the universal process of birth, growth, decay, and death.

—JOSEPH GOLDSTEIN[1]

JAE'S FATHER HAD A STROKE WHEN HE WAS A TEENAGER, SO BOTH he and his sister Stacie knew about the dangers of hypertension and their hereditary risk. Jae was careful, and he maintained a healthy lifestyle as he aged—walking and biking to keep fit, monitoring his blood pressure every month, and becoming the family cook after he married to ensure that he, his wife, and their kids ate low-fat, high-fiber meals. Still, by the time he was thirty-five, his LDL cholesterol was high and his doctor prescribed statins—drugs that are effective in preventing strokes.

On the other hand, Stacie didn't exercise and didn't check in with her doctors for years at a time. She wasn't overweight and didn't smoke, but when she was forty-three, she came downstairs one morning and told her husband that she felt light-headed. He encouraged her to sit on the couch and went to the kitchen to get her a glass of apple juice. When he returned, she was lying on the floor unresponsive. The paramedics got there quickly and treated her for a stroke. The hospital discovered a large clot had burst on the left side of her brain. It would take months of physical and speech therapy before she could walk and talk again. Seeing her so helpless in the intensive care unit, Jae was crushed. He wished he'd nagged her about taking care of herself or reminded her husband that hypertension ran in their family. He remembered how every holiday that they spent together—Thanksgiving, Labor Day, Mother's Day—he wanted her to try his portable blood pressure machine. Sometimes she didn't feel like doing it, and other times he forgot to ask her. Now he felt guilty that he didn't do more to prevent her stroke.

Maria felt guilty too. Her Uncle Alvin died alone in the hospital. His friend Donnie noticed when Alvin didn't arrive at their local diner to eat at the counter like he did nearly every morning, so he walked over to the building and told the super. The super called the police and Maria's mom, and when they got into her uncle's apartment, they found him in his bathroom, delirious from a kidney infection and dehydration. They took him to nearby Elmhurst Hospital and the doctors told them that, with antibiotics and rest, he would likely make a full recovery. But then he contracted a staph infection, which killed him. Maria had been planning to visit him after work one night, but the subway ride was long from her place in Crown Heights in Brooklyn, and she kept putting it off. When her mom called to say he died, she was shocked and sad. And then she felt terrible—selfish, unkind, and stupid—for not visiting him sooner.

If you're thinking about a painful past situation and replaying it over and over in your head and can't seem to stop, you're ruminating. When you notice you're doing it, put your hand on your heart, exhale deeply, and say silently: *May I let go with ease.*

After a loss, it's easy to look back and wish you'd done something differently. So many of us feel like Jae or Maria, filled with regret and blaming ourselves. So often I've heard people say, "Why didn't I see it coming?" or "I should've spent more time with her," or "I wish I'd asked more questions." But looking back like this is a painful delusion because it's impossible for us to have known in the past what was going to happen. We couldn't predict the future or comprehend then what the outcome would be, because the future isn't in our control. Even if Jae had persuaded Stacie to be more careful, there was no guarantee that she would not have had a stroke. Too many causes and conditions created the circumstances of his sister's illness—including genetics and diet—and Jae couldn't control all of it. In the same way, it was impossible for Maria to know that her Uncle Alvin would succumb to an infection so quickly.

An important aspect of wisdom is knowing what you're responsible for and what you're not; you're not responsible for what happens to other people. You can love them and support them and contribute to their happiness and health, but so much more is entirely out of your hands. If you're feeling guilty about something you should have done, remember that the past is more complicated than you remember and that you made the best decisions you could with the information you had at the time.

If you still feel that you made a mistake, it's okay. You can acknowledge it, learn from it, and let it go. There are lessons for all of us in our past behaviors, and we can choose to do things differently in the future, without feeling guilty or ashamed.

In Tibetan Vajrayana Buddhism, there is a ritual called the Four Powers. It's an exercise that we can use when we have regrets about our past behavior that enables us to look at it and let it go.

1. *The Power of Regret.* Acknowledge a negative action. This doesn't mean you're a bad person or you need to beat yourself up about it, but it means acknowledging that you're human, you made a mistake, and you can accept that it was harmful.

2. *The Power of Reliance.* You can reconnect with your beneficial intention simply by putting your hand on your heart and remembering that you want to act wisely and kindly, that you truly wish to speak and act in ways that are useful, loving, and not harmful.

3. *The Power of Resolve.* You make a decision—a choice—not to make the same mistake again. You can do this in the form of a vow, saying: *I vow not to impulsively criticize my son again* or *I vow not to forget to spend time with my sister again.* Put your hand on your heart and repeat your vow to yourself three times.

4. *The Power of the Remedy.* With this final step, you release your guilt and regret. You can light a candle and say: *I forgive myself for making mistakes.* Or you can apologize out loud to the person you've harmed or even make a bow to the universe. The remedy is a symbolic gesture of humility, an understanding that bad actions don't mean you're a bad person and that, just like everyone else, you're doing your best and are committed to doing better.

Practice 21: Self-Forgiveness

Making mistakes—saying the wrong thing, not knowing an answer, or doing something harmful—doesn't mean that we're bad, stupid, or worthless. It just means that we're human. Sadly, many of us have been told or taught that we should strive for perfection, and we beat ourselves up when we don't meet such an impossibly high standard. This meditation, adapted from one by mindfulness teacher Eric Kolvig, can be practiced any time that you wish you'd done, said, or felt something differently.

Remember: if you don't feel you're ready to forgive yourself or anyone else, that's okay. You can simply say: *I have the intention to someday forgive.*

1. Sit or lie down in a quiet, comfortable spot. Turn off your devices and stop talking.

2. Put your hand on your belly and take a few deep breaths, fully exhaling.

3. Imagine something you said or did that you regret, and say these phrases silently to yourself for a few minutes: *I allow myself to be imperfect. I allow myself to make mistakes. I allow myself to be a learner, still learning life's lessons. I forgive myself.*

4. Now take a moment to think of a time when someone hurt or harmed you. Begin with a minor harm, not a terrible or traumatic injury or betrayal. Now say these phrases silently to this person: *I allow you to be imperfect. I allow you to make mistakes. I allow you to be a learner, still learning life's lessons. I forgive you.*

5. Finally, recall a time when you harmed or hurt someone. Offer these phrases silently to this person: *Allow me to be imperfect. Allow me to make mistakes. Allow me to be a learner, still learning life's lessons. Please forgive me.*

6. Take ten breaths before you end the meditation, and be sure to thank yourself and appreciate your wisdom and efforts.

CHAPTER 22

When You're Lost and Afraid

According to the Buddha, "You can search throughout the entire universe for someone who is more deserving of your love and affection than you are yourself, and that person is not to be found anywhere. You yourself, as much as anybody in the entire universe, deserve your love and affection."

—SHARON SALZBERG[1]

ABOUT FIVE MONTHS AFTER MY MOTHER DIED, I WAS STILL DEPRESSED, anxious, and unsteady. I was doing everything I knew to do—going to yoga, seeing a therapist, and having bodywork regularly—and I still felt awful. I was in despair and considered moving to Lori's house in Chicago and living in her spare room. Then I went on a weeklong meditation retreat at the Insight Meditation Society in Barre, Massachusetts. With a hundred people, I sat in a meditation hall contemplating my breath and offering myself and others loving-kindness. I hiked on the frosty paths in the surrounding forest and got up early for a predawn breakfast. For the first two days I was restless and worried. Late in the afternoon on the third day while doing walking meditation in a quiet hallway, I felt something shift in my chest—like my heart breaking. It felt so painful but I was relieved to feel it. I realized that I'd been holding in so much sadness. As I cried, I realized that nothing was wrong at all. It was perfectly okay to feel like this because I could see that underneath all my upset there was a clear and steady presence that was unshakable and peaceful. I knew with certainty that even after the retreat ended and I returned to my apartment and my regular life, I would get through this difficult time and heal.

And I did, and so will you.

There might be moments during your grief when you feel you don't know what is going to happen to you, how you're going to get through it, or if things will get worse. After Mabel's husband committed suicide, she was frightened all the time, jumped at every noise, and stayed awake until dawn. When her friends Jean and Jim came for dinner one night with their little dog Sassy, Mabel felt so lonely saying goodnight to them that she cried as she watched their car pull out of the driveway. Ten minutes later she heard a strange rustling at her door but couldn't see anything. She sat down at the kitchen table frozen with fear. She thought she must finally be losing her mind. The sound continued and she even imagined she heard sobbing. When the doorbell rang, she looked out the window and saw Jean stooping to pick up Sassy. The dog hadn't gotten in the car when they left, and what she'd thought was frightening and mysterious was Sassy scratching at her door to come inside.

> If you're feeling so disturbed that you're having thoughts of harming yourself or anyone else, it doesn't mean you're crazy. It means you're under tremendous stress—like many of us—and need professional guidance and care. You're not alone. Reach out to a friend or professional immediately, and/or contact one of the organizations in the Resources section at the end of the book.

Please know that you're not alone in feeling terrible and that you will not always feel this way. If you believe you can't take it anymore during dark moments when you feel unsteady, anguished, or afraid, be assured that it will not last forever—there will be a time when you feel steady, less overwhelmed, and more like your old self. Although a great loss causes many changes, the quiet, wise, kind part of you always is present, even if it's obscured by heartbreak and misery right now. Also know that you're not crazy and you don't have to hide what you're going through—there are many professionals and bereavement groups that can offer you support and provide you with tools and skills to help you care for yourself.

Serena wasn't sure if she would ever feel like herself again. She developed chronic pain after she fractured her pelvis when she fell while trying to cut an old branch from the mulberry tree in her backyard. For the first two years after the accident, she spent as much time trying to bodily heal—doing physical therapy and learning to walk again—as she did mourning her old life. She cried continually, less from pain than from frustration that she—once an active retired person, a gardener and a good cook who enjoyed traveling and sang in the church choir—was so limited that walking more than ten minutes was so painful and exhausting that she had to sit down. But Serena's family encouraged her to use her resources wisely, and she talked to the minister at her church and joined an online group for chronic pain. Slowly, she felt less depressed. Her church reading group came to her house for its monthly meeting, she learned to use Zoom to talk with friends, and she allowed herself to enjoy a slower paced life and more time alone with her husband. As she said recently with a smile, "It took me a while, but now I feel good enough is good enough."

The Buddhist Three Marks of Existence are distinct attributes that define all human experience. These characteristics are:

- unsatisfactoriness
- impermanence
- not-self

It's easy to understand the truth of unsatisfactoriness—we all can see that no matter what happens to us, we still have discontentment, desires, or want things to be different. And impermanence is obvious—nothing that happens lasts or stays the same. But not-self is trickier to understand. Translated from the Pali word *anatta*, not-self means that anything that happens to us is not an experience of a solid, unchanging self or identity. Rather, our self is actually an ever-changing dynamic entity, responding and adapting to new situations and different stages of life, arising to meet the unpredictable circumstances and conditions of each moment.

The fact that we don't have a frozen, fixed self is a good thing. It means that we don't have to cling to ideas about who we are—we can allow ourselves to be different, to evolve, and to change. For example, for a long time, I thought of myself as a "good sleeper." I told friends I was lucky to be a good sleeper—falling asleep easily, never having insomnia, and rarely waking during the night. But during the pandemic, I had trouble sleeping. I realized that I had never been a good sleeper—it was just that for a long time I enjoyed the conditions that allowed me to sleep well. When those conditions changed, my experience changed too. All of us have ideas like this about who we are, and that's okay, but if we refuse to allow ourselves to change because we think we have a fixed identity that we have to hold on to, then we'll feel bad about ourselves and our circumstances when life changes. We'll feel like we've lost something essential instead of just losing an idea. Recognizing the truth of not-self—that none of us will always be a bad dancer, a spouse, a lawyer, an excellent speaker, a person who is always on time— liberates us from having to be a certain way all the time. Everything is impermanent and ever changing—including us—and when we make peace with not-self, we're free to be whoever we are right this moment, without regret, denial, or anger.

Practice 22: You Got through It

This exercise helps you remember all the many difficult times in your life when you've had to solve a problem, deal with a disappointment, or even put your life back together after a big transition. When you're struggling with the uncertainty and upset of change and loss and worried what will happen and how you'll get through it, it can be helpful to compile a "got-through-it" list.

Write down a list of difficult experiences, adversities, changes, or losses that you experienced in the past, how you got through them, who helped you, and how you felt. My got-through-it list includes the time my cat fell out of a five-story window and lived and all the neighbors who helped him; my life in my twenties without a college degree and working as a waitress, unsure of what to do or where to go; how pained and confused I was after my mom died and all the healers who helped me through it; and a breakup with a serious boyfriend in my thirties and how hard it was to start over as a single person again.

As you make your got-through-it list, you'll see that you've experienced some difficult struggles in the past. You got through them then, and you can reassure yourself that no matter how hard things are now, you'll get through this too. Your-got-through-it list might also help you realize that you have the tools and the support to meet difficulties and challenges with skill, kindness, and self-compassion because you've done it many times before.

After you've written your list, take a moment to close your eyes, put your hand on your heart, and say silently: *May I remember to have faith in myself to find the help I need to get through this challenging time.*

CHAPTER 23

Mourning and Social Media

Better than a thousand useless words is one useful word, upon hearing which one attains peace.

—THE BUDDHA[1]

WHEN YOU'RE GRIEVING, YOU MIGHT FEEL PARTICULARLY SENSITIVE. Sometimes you might be glad for the support of online friends, and other times you might feel overwhelmed with their condolences or advice. Family members might insist on oversharing or make it seem like their grief is greater than yours. Taking care of yourself includes being mindful of the time you spend on social media and practicing wise communication—remembering that you can't control what others say or do, but you can choose to use your words wisely and kindly.

This wasn't easy for Mary after her father, Tim, was treated for prostate cancer and went into remission for more than five years. When his illness returned, it had spread to his bladder and the prognosis wasn't great—it was Stage 4 and aggressive. She sat with her stepmother Janet and her brother David in the hallway of a North Carolina hospital, clutching a paper cup with cold coffee while Janet cried and begged the doctor to save "my hero, my husband." Mary and David liked Janet—she'd been married to their dad for nearly twenty years—but the siblings often felt that she overshared and gossiped, and they'd learned not to say much of real importance to her. As a result, Janet felt like an outsider, believing they kept secrets from her. Now, in this cold corridor, Mary and David were annoyed with Janet's histrionics but determined to do their best to support their dad, which meant supporting Janet too.

> If you're not sure whether you should comment or post on social media, don't. Wait at least ten minutes and check in with yourself again. If you're feeling more confident, go ahead and share. Otherwise, do nothing.

Mary lived in Virginia, where she and David had grown up, and she'd left her three children and husband to drive to the hospital in Raleigh the night before her dad's surgery. Her middle child, eleven-year-old Lizzie, was her father's favorite, and Mary decided she would wait until she returned home to tell her about her grandpa's illness. Their relationship surprised Mary because her dad wasn't really interested in children. When she and David were young, he practiced a form of benign neglect until they were teenagers, and he showed similar interest in her other kids and David's son too. Mary knew Lizzie was worried and hoped her dad would soon be well enough to talk to her himself.

The doctors said that it was likely her dad would be discharged the next day, and David planned to leave afterward. Mary would help Janet get her dad home and settled, and if all went well, in forty-eight hours, she would get in her car and drive home. Both Mary and David were staying at their dad and Janet's house, a three-bedroom in a new, fifty-plus community next to the golf course. Mary and David were glad to have a place to stay, and after a dinner of Chinese takeout, they left Janet texting with her friends on an iPad while watching television in the great room. Mary was relieved when she closed the door to the back bedroom that looked out on the green after saying goodnight to David, who continued to the smaller guest room next to the kitchen.

After Mary called and talked with her family, she fell asleep with her phone in her hand while texting her cousin. She was propped up on a decorative bolster against the headboard, the lights on, dozing when David sat down on the bed and said, "Did you see this?" and held up his phone. She read Janet's Facebook post, "My hero husband's cancer is back, this time in his bladder. We are going to fight this. Please pray for Tim and our family <3, <3, <3." "Where's my phone?" Mary said, fumbling with the bedspread. "I better call Lizzie before someone else tells her about this."

Social media is a double-edged sword—it keeps us in touch with our friends and family, but too many of us have experienced the upset or hurt resulting from ill-considered and insensitive posts. In Buddhism, the practice of wise communication is called skillful speech, and we can use it to guide all of our interactions—including conversation, phone calls, texts, letters, and social media—to help us use our words to benefit and not do harm. Skillful speech includes being honest and not misleading, refraining from divisive speech (like gossip), not speaking abusively or with hostility, and not talking in a meaningless, idle way. It also means knowing when to speak and when not to speak—or in the case of social media, knowing when to share or not to share.

Julie wasn't sure how to respond after she wrote what she thought was a polite post on Facebook. A medical receptionist, she'd lost her job at the chiropractic office when her location closed and thought that her social network might help her find a new position. Although most of her Facebook friends were encouraging, several people wrote cruel and insulting comments. "How many times have you been fired already?" Another said, "What are you complaining about? At least you can get unemployment—I don't even got that." The final insult came when her cousin wrote, "Don't expect me to feel sorry for you, everybody has problems."

All of us can remember moments in our lives when a stranger said something kind and we felt touched, and also those moments when a loved one said something careless and we were hurt. The words we say and how we say them matter because they affect whoever hears or reads them and we can choose to impact others positively or negatively. We now have so many mediums with which to communicate—email, websites, film, texts, social media—that we're able to affect more people than ever before, which is why it's especially important today to practice skillful speech.

The easiest way to do this is to pause. Taking time before you say or write something ensures that you don't react out of upset or excitement. Instead, take the time to consider if your communication will be useful and wise. If not—if it's unnecessary, untrue, or mean—you don't have to say it or write anything at all. In Mary's case, she chose not to write any comments on her stepmother's Facebook post. Instead, the next morning she politely asked Janet to wait before posting any more news about her dad so that the grandchildren and other family members wouldn't be surprised. For Julie, she was so hurt that she considered deleting her post entirely, but she took a friend's advice and sat down and felt her feelings. She noticed how defensive she felt, and her impulse was to explain her situation or to hurt the commentors the way they hurt her. Instead, she decided not to do anything for twenty-four hours. The next day, she decided she would reply with thanks—but only for the useful and kind comments she'd received. The insulting and mean comments, she ignored.

> Skillful speech is one of the disciplines of the Eightfold Path, a Buddhist road map for living in harmony with yourself and others. Included in the Buddha's very first teaching, these eight practices orient our minds and behavior toward beneficial action and help us to prevent harming ourselves and each other. The practices include skillful speech, livelihood, action, effort, mindfulness, concentration, understanding, and intention. All encourage us to use our words, thoughts, and behaviors with wisdom and compassion so that we don't cause suffering to ourselves or others. The Eightfold Path reminds us that sometimes the wisest action is none at all.

Practice 23: Skillful Speech

Facebook, Instagram, Twitter, and all the other ways of communicating through social media and technology can be fraught with misunderstandings, hurt feelings, meanness, and oversharing. Using these platforms skillfully requires mindfulness, and if you're grieving or upset, you may need to be especially careful with such online communications. Below are a few guidelines to consider before posting or sharing information about you or your feelings online:

1. Be aware of the time you spend online and limit it. Set a maximum number of minutes or hours and follow it. You might choose to look at your phone only once an hour for up to five minutes or make it a rule to look at social media only in the evening for half an hour. Choosing the duration of social media use prevents you from thoughtlessly getting swept away or inadvertently causing harm or being harmed.

2. Before you post, comment, or write a review, take time to do the following.

   • Pause. Don't post for at least ten minutes.

   • During the pause, notice what is arising in you. Are you angry, needy, or confused? Take a few deep breaths to give yourself patience. Don't post until you feel calm and clearheaded.

   • After the pause, ask yourself what your intention is. What outcome do you want to bring about through your post? Do you want to share information to help others? Do you want to tell someone they're wrong or stupid? Do you want others simply to hear your opinion? If your intention is harmful or upsetting, you might decide not to post or share anything.

3. When you're clear about why you're communicating and that your intention isn't harmful, you're ready to post. Or you might find—as I often do—that after you take a pause, you discover that you don't need to say anything at all.

CHAPTER 24

Letting Life Unfold—Going Forward

Nothing endures but change, and accepting this has the potential to transform the dread of dying into joyful living.
—YONGEY MINGYUR RINPOCHE[1]

A DECADE AGO, I WAS STANDING ON A YOGA MAT, BENDING MY HEAD over my knees at Ishta Yoga on 11th Street near Union Square, when someone's cell phone began ringing loudly from the back of the studio on the shelf where students stashed their belongings. The teacher ignored it and continued guiding us into the next posture, but the phone continued to ring. The other fifteen people in class and I looked around surreptitiously, trying to see when and who would claim the phone and shut it off. Annoyingly, no one did, and it finally stopped ringing. But a few minutes later when we were standing on one leg in tree pose, it rang again. This time, Douglass, our teacher, looked around the room as the rest of us pursed our lips and narrowed our eyes, irritated by the rude interruption and impatiently wondering why the phone's owner didn't shut it off.

When the phone rang for the third time, Douglass had just instructed us in a wide-leg forward bend, and I sat astride my mat, reaching my arms away from my body, stretching my fingertips toward the door, about to lean forward, when I suddenly recognized the ringtone. It was the same alarm I'd set to remind myself to call my doctor yesterday. Did I forget to shut it off? I abruptly got to my feet, stammered loudly, "Oh my god, that's my phone," and tiptoed between the mats to the back of the room, where I snatched my tote from the cubby, turned off the alarm, and powered down my phone. I sheepishly returned to my mat, embarrassed, and mouthed "I'm sorry" to Douglass, who smiled.

> Death is something we avoid talking about, though it's a definite fact of life. If you're feeling dread or terror about death and dying, don't be impatient with yourself but don't indulge your fears either. Learn to make peace with impermanence through mindfulness, compassion, and loving-kindness using the techniques in this book and connecting with other spiritual traditions too.

The class couldn't know it, but I was grieving. My mom had died just a few weeks before, and I didn't feel like myself at all—I was spacey, forgetful, and tired. Already I'd lost my keys twice—once I found them at the counter of the deli where I got my fig bars and a few days later my neighbor found them hanging on my box in the mailroom, still in the lock, and returned them to me. Several times I was late for work because I missed my stop on the subway and had to double back. So when my loud cell phone alarm rang during yoga class, it took me a while to realize that it was mine, but I wasn't surprised.

People once grieved openly and for a long time, signifying that they were in mourning so that others could offer them patience and empathy (in some cultures, they still do, but in our contemporary American society, outward mourning lasts a week or two at most). For nearly two years after the death of a spouse or child, Victorian Europeans wore black. In India and China, they wore white for up to a year. But today in the United States, the average company's human resources policy permits between one and five days off for a death in the family. The federal government still refers to bereavement leave as "funeral leave," completely disregarding the space and time—weeks, months, and in many cases, years—necessary to mourn. That's why now, when I hear a cell phone ring where it shouldn't—at the theater, a concert, a movie—I no longer think "What a jerk!" or "Why didn't you shut off your phone?" Instead, I now wonder if that person's mom died and say silently, "May you be peaceful and at ease."

If you're going through a loss right now, although you might wish with all of your might that it hadn't happened the way it did, the reality is that it *did* happen. Now you have a choice: you can allow this loss to harden you and close your heart, or you can connect with your grief and sorrow and let it help you meet the unfolding of life with greater kindness and openness for yourself and for all those you encounter. Although it's true you'll never be the same again, it doesn't mean that you'll never feel happy, whole, or hopeful. You can use your experience as an opportunity to recognize the wisdom of impermanence, to orient your life in meaningful endeavors, and to use your energy toward compassionate action for you and for all those you encounter.

Months after Denise died, on my way to our local park, I saw a dead bird on the sidewalk. As I got nearer, I looked down at it, and the bird blinked. I realized she—it was female—wasn't dead. Unsure what to do, I took off my sweatshirt and gently but securely wrapped it around the bird and sat her upright near the curb. She blinked and moved a bit, and as I looked for a box or a bag to transport her to the Wildbird Fund—a veterinary rescue group that heals and rehabilitates birds in New York City—she wriggled out of the shirt, rustled her wings, and flew into the air. I watched with open-mouthed delight as she took wing into the trees and wondered if it was my old friend, my heart overflowing with inexpressible joy and gratitude for this bird's life, my life, and all our lives. It's my deepest intention and wish that this book inspires the same sense of appreciation in you and that its practices guide you when you're lost, comfort you when you're down, and provide a foundation from which your loving intention to benefit yourself and others takes root in your heart and flourishes.

Soon after I began writing this book, my father died. For nearly a year, unable to walk and his dementia worsening, he'd required twenty-four-hour care. A week before he passed, his caregiver Elizabeth told me he would likely die soon, so I went to his home and sat at his bedside for the last two days of his life. It had been more than ten years since my mother died, and I was surprised that I wasn't falling apart or in shock. Instead, I was grateful and sad as I watched his frail, old body fade. He'd lost consciousness, and his inhalations were loud and labored, his exhalations hissing through his open, dry mouth. I knew he wasn't going to recover, yet it didn't quite seem possible that he would not be alive.

As I permitted the truth of impermanence to enter my mind, I also viscerally realized that someday I too would no longer be alive. I felt in my heart how brief and precious life is and a deep sense of urgency that I needed to prioritize what was important to me from that moment on. For me, this meant focusing my energy and time on my husband, my family, and my work as a meditation teacher. It also meant recommitting myself as a Buddhist student, and I repeated my intention out loud to my dad, saying, "I want to be free and I want everyone—including you—to be free too." Then I remembered an old sutta—a teaching directly from the historic Buddha—that explains that whatever is saved from a fire is useful and whatever is left behind is destroyed and has no value. It's a parable to encourage us to give away our most valuable possessions—our love, compassion, wisdom, generosity, patience, and joy. Since they're of no use to anyone when we're dead, we should give them away to benefit ourselves and all beings while we're alive.

The Aditta Sutta

When your house is on fire,
you rescue the pot
that's useful,
not the one that's burnt.
And as the world is on fire
with old age and death,
you should rescue by giving,
for what's given is rescued.[2]

Practice 24: Give It All Away

A beautiful way to develop generosity is to imagine yourself giving away *everything*. With this contemplative practice, you're asked to visualize yourself giving your possessions, your body, your beautiful qualities, and your environment—even the earth—to others. It requires us to practice mindfulness by noticing all that we have, which develops our gratitude. Through gratitude we recognize that we have so much that we can offer it to others, which cultivates generosity. And with generosity, we are free from the greed, neediness, and fear that arises from our confused attachments and clinging, so our minds become happy, clear, and wise.

1. Begin by finding a quiet place where you can be undisturbed. Turn off your devices, close your eyes or gaze softly at the ground, put your hand on your heart, and take a few deep breaths.

2. Close your eyes and take a mental inventory of your most important material possessions, any money or investments, a car or a house, a beloved family heirloom, a favorite book. Now imagine giving them away—to people you love, friends, strangers, those in need. You can picture yourself making the offering and the delight of those who receive it. You don't have to worry about giving it to the most deserving person or spend too much time choosing the perfect gift. What's important is the act of giving.

3. After you've given away your material possessions, make a mental inventory of your beautiful qualities. Recall examples of your kindness, generosity, patience, love, compassion, joy, wisdom,

and any other beneficial attributes. Then imagine giving those away, too—to people you love, friends, strangers, even your enemies who might be most in need.

4. After you've given away your beautiful qualities, imagine nature. Visualize the trees, plants, oceans, air, volcanos—the earth itself—and give it all away. Not to one person or a single group, but to all living beings impartially. You can think: *I offer our home, the planet earth, to everyone. May all beings benefit from my gift of the earth.*

5. After you are done giving, rest in silence. Take a few moments to notice your body, your heart, and your breath. Before ending this contemplation, silently say to yourself: *I offer my gratitude for the life I have been given.*

CHAPTER 25

Honoring Loss

I could not count the times during the average day when something would come up that I needed to tell him. This impulse did not end with his death. What ended was the possibility of response.

—JOAN DIDION[1]

WALKING HOME FROM THE SUBWAY ABOUT A MONTH AFTER DENISE died, my body felt so heavy and my mind was filled with images of her when she was sick, memories of our vacations in Fair Harbor, and the sounds of her cat crying when I took him to his new home with our friends in Brooklyn. The feeling of heartache was so heavy and tight in my chest and throat and my mind was so distressed and upset that I realized it would be less painful to cut off my arm or my leg than it was to lose someone I love. But as I approached my building with its garden lights flickering in the autumn dusk, it occurred to me that even if I could somehow—magically—make my sorrow vanish, remove my grief, I wouldn't do it. I couldn't imagine anything more terrible than losing someone dear without it affecting me at all—this seemed far worse than the most agonizing mourning. I decided then that it was neither a burden nor an obligation to grieve my friend, but rather an honor, and I was privileged to carry the memory of her life and the impact of her deeds. I also understood why death rituals are found throughout all cultures, because remembering the deceased and acknowledging their importance can help us process, understand, and move through our bereavement.

Although it can feel like the world should stop turning altogether, life doesn't stop after you experience an ending. Externally, nothing has changed—the presidential election is held, the snow falls then melts, the new employees need to be trained—but everything has changed *for you*. Ritual is a way to appreciate your loss, pay tribute to the past, and celebrate life—your own and that of your deceased loved one.

> If you feel there is nothing you can do after someone dies, remember that you can always pray. Even if you're an atheist, offering a simple blessing to the deceased like, "May you be held in goodness," is a useful antidote for helplessness and despair, and it doesn't require you to ask God to intercede—it's just a sincere wish from you, generously offered from your heart.

There are many ways to create a personal ritual for your loss. If you have a religion or a faith tradition, you might follow its ceremonies by saying prayers, holding a Catholic mass, or sitting a Jewish shiva or a Hindu Śrāddha. In many places in the world, holidays and celebrations honor the dead—Japan celebrates Obon each year to remember and venerate ancestors, as does China, which calls its holiday the Ghost Festival, and in Mexico, it is the annual Day of the Dead.

Many Buddhists believe in reincarnation—that each of us is reborn after death as a different creature—a human, an insect, a catfish, or another living being. In some countries, like Thailand, they believe that it takes one hundred days to reincarnate, and in others, like Tibet, the tradition says it takes up to forty-nine days after death to be reborn. During this time, prayers are said for the deceased to protect them on their journey between lives, to reassure them that they are safe and loved, and to wish them an auspicious new life. On the last day, a ceremony is held for friends and family to say goodbye and to offer their blessings.

If you don't have a religion or faith, you can still benefit from ritual, and there are many ways to create your own. When my mom died, I adapted the Tibetan forty-nine-day tradition, which I share in the following practice. You can personalize it for your mourning period too. After Denise died, I created a small altar for her on top of a bookshelf in the living room, where I put photos of her and us, her favorite books, cards and letters she wrote to me, and gifts she'd given to me. Each night I lit a candle and said a brief prayer for her—and many evenings, I still do. When Melvin's son died, he kept a remembrance journal, and each day he wrote something about Cary and included his gratitude for their relationship. Anything that supports you in your bereavement can be your ritual—you can take a silent walk each week in memory of your dear one or stay at home for several days after their death, spending time in reflection and contemplation and refraining from mundane activities like television and the internet.

Rituals don't have to be ceremonial, spiritual, or religious. A few weeks after his old Labrador Pippen died, John's wife suggested they get a new puppy from the shelter, but John wasn't ready. He had a special relationship with Pippen and didn't want to feel like he was trying to replace him or avoid his grief with the excitement of a young, cute dog. When John thought about how he could best pay tribute to Pippen's kindness and loyalty, he created his own ritual. Every Friday before work, he drove to PAWS Animal Rescue and walked one of their shelter dogs. It made him feel happy to pay forward a little bit of the sweetness he'd received from his own beloved dog. One day, about six months later, he walked a four-year-old collie-lab mutt who gave him such a soulful look when they returned to PAWS after their walk that he went home and told his wife he'd found their new dog. They took Jordan home that weekend.

In some Buddhist countries, it's believed that the best way to support the dead is to give them our merit. Merit—sometimes translated as virtue or luck—is generated whenever we perform good or wholesome deeds, which include kind thoughts, wise and gentle speech, and skillful and loving actions. In several Southeast Asian countries, it's traditional for bereaved families to pay for a meal for all the monastics at the temple, where the merit from this generous act is dedicated to their loved one. You can give your merit away, too, by learning to be mindful whenever you say or do something that's for the benefit of others. If you stop your car to let a stranger pull out of a parking spot or if you babysit your sister's kids so she can go to a job interview, you can say silently, "I give any merit or luck from my kindness to my dear [name]." In this way, any kindness you share is also an opportunity to connect with the dead.

Practice 25: The Forty-Ninth-Day Ritual

Some Buddhist traditions believe it takes up to forty-nine days after death for someone to reincarnate into another being, and until that time, daily prayers are offered to protect the dead and to reassure them that they are loved. Then, on the forty-ninth day, a memorial service is held to say goodbye and wish the deceased well in their new life.

Most people I know aren't very religious, and even if they are, the ceremonies and services of contemporary traditions—funerals, pujas, memorials—usually take place soon after death—within a week or two at most. After that, we're all on our own, expected to get back to normal and work through our grief privately. When I held a forty-ninth-day gathering after my mom died, I realized that it's a useful amount of time—about six weeks after a loss—when mourners are still feeling lonely, lost, and in need of support, although other people in our lives may have moved on.

Doing a forty-ninth-day ritual doesn't mean that you believe in reincarnation, God, Buddha, or anything at all. You can do it to honor your own sadness, love, and tenderness, and you can organize it however you like. You can choose to light a candle, say a prayer, write a note, set a place at your table, or say the name of your loved one every day. Or you can create your own ritual and do it once a week whenever you feel like it. You can also make a donation in honor of that person or volunteer for a cause that was important to them.

On the forty-ninth day, you can organize a gathering in celebration and commemoration of the deceased. This can be formal or casual, large or small, and you can meet in a temple, a restaurant, at home, or even on Zoom. Ask everyone to share a memory or a photo, or put together a slideshow tribute of the person's life. You can also ask everyone to join in an aspiration prayer, which is a hope extended from your hearts to your loved one. You can use one of the prayers below or write your own. Finally, don't forget to dedicate the merit—offering the goodness created from your collective caring, sharing, and love—to your dear one: *We offer any merit arising from our forty-ninth-day gathering to our dear [name]. May [he or she or they] be safe and free and dwell in happy realms. May we meet again in many lifetimes.*

Aspiration Prayers

You can all read both or either of these prayers in a group, or one person can say a line followed by the group repeating it in unison. Repeat each prayer three times.

> *We rejoice in our relationship with you.*
> *We offer you our love and blessings.*
> *May we meet again through many lifetimes.*
> *May we awaken and be free.*
> *May it be so!*

> *Thank you for your love and friendship.*
> *May you be happy and at ease.*
> *May we know the great peace that we are.*
> *May it be so!*

Mindfulness Meditation Instructions

Mindfulness meditation is a simple technique of being present with whatever is happening inside and outside of you during each moment. By bringing your attention to what's occurring right now, you'll be less consumed with worries about the future or regrets about the past. You'll be able to be with whatever is in your mind, body, and heart, whether you like it, dislike it, or find it dull, and to develop your capacity to react less out of habit and more from choice and good sense. Anyone can practice mindfulness. It doesn't require special equipment, it's not religious, and it can be done anywhere. I suggest practicing these instructions for fifteen minutes each day.

Step 1: Get Still

Sit, stand, or lie down somewhere that is relatively quiet where you won't be interrupted. comfortably keeping your hands still. Get as comfortable as possible, with a straight spine and breathing easily, in a chair or a cushion on the floor. Eyes can be open or closed.

Step 2: Say Hello

Take a minute or two to ask yourself, "How *am* I right now?" A response may come in the form of words, images, and/or bodily sensations—simply notice what surfaces but try not to get too caught up in it. Allowing whatever is arising to emerge can help us approach our body and mind with compassion.

STEP 3: COME TO YOUR SENSES

Bring your attention to your body, noticing your feet touching the ground, your seat, the palms of your hands, experiencing your shoulder blades, the back of your head, allowing sound to enter your ears.

STEP 4: FIND AN ANCHOR

Choose an object of attention on which to focus. This is most commonly the breath, but you can use sounds or the feeling of your feet touching the floor. If using the breath, find one place in your body where you can feel your inhalations and exhalations: the tip of your nose, your abdomen, your chest. Experience the sensations and movement of your body breathing, and allow it to anchor you in the present moment.

It's very common to notice that attention stays with the breath or body for only a few cycles before it wanders away. If you notice your mind remembering or planning something, see if you can simply come back to *this one breath that you are breathing right at this moment.* Don't worry if you have to do this a hundred times in a single meditation session. Each time you bring yourself gently back to your breath, you are strengthening your concentration—the ability to direct your mind back to the present moment.

STEP 5: SAY THANK YOU

At the end of the meditation session, take a moment to appreciate and acknowledge the benefits of the practice you just did—not only for yourself, but for everyone you have contact with that day.

Appendix B

Metta Meditation Instructions

METTA MEDITATION IS A BUDDHIST PRACTICE DESIGNED TO HELP you cultivate concentration, wisdom, and compassion. *Metta* is a Pali (the language of the early Buddhist texts) word that translates to "friendship" or "loving-kindness" or "love." But the intention of offering *metta* is to develop your loving heart by connecting with other beings and recognizing their wish to be happy, their desire not to suffer, and their deep struggles. *Metta* meditation is traditionally offered to five beings in a progressive order from easiest to love to the hardest; the order is self, beloved benefactor, dear friend, familiar stranger, and someone you dislike. Note that you may experience love, happiness, sadness, annoyance, crabbiness, boredom, or any other feelings during this meditation. This is normal and you don't need to chase or create "positive" emotions. Any time you notice that you've lost the connection with the person or the phrases, gently return your attention to the practice and begin again.

Traditional *metta* phrases include:

May I/you/we be safe.

May I/you/we be happy.

May I/you/we be healthy.

May I/you/we live with ease.

Step 1: Find a comfortable place to sit on a chair or a cushion on the floor. Close your eyes or open them softly and stare at the floor. Bring your attention to the physical sensations of your body: notice sounds entering your ears, the feeling of your feet, the sensation of your breath as it rises and falls in your belly, light entering your eyelids. Pay attention to coolness, tension or tightness, warmth, pulsing, or even pain. You don't have to change anything or fix anything, just patiently notice what's arising.

Step 2: Bring your attention to anchor in the center of your chest at your heart. Allow a sense of yourself to arise. This could be an image of you as an adult or as a child; it may be a sense of your own presence in your heart. When you've made this connection to yourself, offer the phrases silently, as though you're giving yourself a gift: *May I be safe, may I be happy, may I be healthy, may I live with ease.* Continue to silently offer these phrases, and if you stray from the words, simply notice this, re-anchor to your sense of yourself, and start the phrases again.

Step 3: Move your attention away from this sense of yourself and the phrases and repeat steps 1 and 2 for each of the remaining four beings: beloved benefactor, dear friend, familiar stranger, and someone you dislike. At the end of the meditation, take a moment to offer *metta* to all beings.

Appendix C

Protection Prayer for the Dead

ADAPTED FROM THE BRAHMAVIHARA PARITTA, A TRADITIONAL BUDDHIST dedication.

STEP 1: MAKING A CONNECTION TO YOUR GOOD HEART
Close your eyes, take a few deep breaths, and notice sounds, smells, and the air around you.

STEP 2: OFFERING YOUR GOODNESS
Repeat the following three times:

> *May I be happy.*
> *May I be free from stress and pain.*
> *May I be free from animosity.*
> *May I be free from oppression.*
> *May I be free from trouble.*
> *May I look after myself with ease.*
>
> *May all living beings be free from animosity.*
> *May all living beings be free from oppression.*
> *May all living beings be free from trouble.*
> *May all living beings look after themselves with ease.*
>
> *May all living beings be free from all stress and suffering and disease. May all beings live happily, always free from animosity.*

Step 3: Giving the Blessings of Your Goodness to the Deceased

Take a deep breath and remember your deceased loved one. Repeat the following:

> *May* [name of deceased] *share in the blessings, springing from the good I have done.*
> *May* [name of deceased] *have every good blessing.*
> *May the devas protect* [her or him].
> *By the power of all the Buddhas, may* [name of deceased] *forever be well.*
>
> *May* [name of deceased] *have every good blessing.*
> *May the devas protect* [her or him].
> *By the power of all the Dhamma, may* [name of deceased] *forever be well.*
>
> *May* [name of deceased] *have every good blessing.*
> *May the devas protect* [her or him].
> *By the power of all Sangha, may* [name of deceased] *forever be well.*
>
> *May we meet again in many lifetimes.*
> *May it be so.*

Step 4: Sealing Your Intention

Sit silently for a few moments. Notice your feelings and your breath. Take your time, and when you're ready, open your eyes and the blessing is complete.

Appendix D

Comforting Grief Meditation

MANY PEOPLE HAVE A MISPERCEPTION ABOUT MEDITATION. THEY want to learn it as a way to change themselves—as a way to get rid of difficult thoughts or stressful feelings or to be more productive or less absentminded. Meditation, however, is a way to change how we relate to ourselves—it's not a way to bypass difficulties or to ignore our human experiences. With meditation, we learn to accommodate every aspect of experience—our hope, fear, delight, rage, calm, agony—with kindness, wisdom, and tenderness.

In *Navigating Grief and Loss*, the intention is to help you become a good friend to yourself—so *you* can console yourself. As you begin to relate to your mourning and loss with patience and gentleness, you'll realize that it isn't a penance or a punishment that you have to *endure*, but rather a profound and poignant human event that you can experience with understanding and self-compassion and that only you can ease your worries, embrace your heartache, and soothe your hurt.

1. Find a quiet spot where you feel secure and comfortable. You can sit in your favorite chair or on the floor, lie down on the couch or your bed, or walk slowly in your hallway or backyard. You can cover yourself with your favorite blanket or throw, turn the lights up or down, and open or close a window. Take your time to create a cozy spot where you can allow yourself to relax

just a little bit. If you feel it's impossible for you to rest, then make yourself a cup of tea and sit down at your kitchen table.

2. Put your devices in another room or shut them down entirely. Turn off your television and the radio, and let your roommates or family know that you don't want to be disturbed. Stop talking. You might feel uncomfortable without the input of the internet or external sounds, and that's okay. Just give yourself permission to be here for ten or twenty minutes.

3. Place your right hand on your belly, around or just below your navel, beneath your shirt or waistband, so you're touching your own skin. Place your left hand on top of your right, and gently let your hands rest on your belly as it rises when you inhale and falls when you exhale. Bring all your attention here, experiencing your breath.

4. Your thoughts might distract you from your breath and your belly. You might find you're in a memory of the past, a plan about the future, or lost in an imaginary conversation. When you notice this, gently move your attention back to your breath and the feeling of your hands. It's normal for thoughts to arise—images, ideas, emotions, regrets, excitement—so you don't need to judge them or wish they weren't happening. All you need to do is choose to bring your awareness back to your belly and your breath, again and again. Stay here for at least five minutes but for as long as you like before moving to the next step.

5. Now take your left hand and place it on your heart, leaving your right hand on your belly. Exhale loudly with a sigh. Do this a few times. You might notice tension or tightness or heaviness in your body, and emotions like sadness, fear, upset, or exhaustion. Keeping your hands on yourself, you can say these sentences silently, *May I be at peace with what's happen-*

ing. May I be a good friend to myself. You can also offer yourself reassuring phrases like "I'm here for you," or "I'm struggling right now and it's okay," or whatever words are comforting and reassuring to you. Stay here for at least five minutes but for as long as you like before moving to the next step.

6. Bring your attention back to your breath, taking a few conscious inhalations and exhalations. Gently scan your body, noticing your head, eyes, cheeks, jaw, throat, arms, hands, heart, belly, abdomen, seat, thighs, lower legs, and feet.

7. Let yourself rest right here and now. You don't have to focus on your breath or on a particular place in your body; instead, just notice your breathing, the sounds entering your ears, and the feeling of your clothing on your skin. If your thoughts sweep you away from the present moment, gently let go and redirect your attention to what you're directly experiencing.

8. You can rest here for as long as you like, and you can repeat the steps as needed, any time. Before you get up, take a moment to appreciate the love and care you've offered yourself, and acknowledge your intention to understand your grief and heal.

NOTES

EPIGRAPHS
1. Adichie, Chimamanda Ngozi, "Notes on Grief," *The New Yorker*, 5 September 2020, www.newyorker.com/culture/personal-history/notes-on-grief.
2. Zenju Earthlyn Manuel, 11 June 2015, https://zenju.org/the-dance-of-death/ (accessed 13 December 2021).

CHAPTER 1. THERE IS NOTHING WRONG WITH YOU
1. Rainer Maria Rilke, "Go to the Limits of Your Longing," *Rilke's Book of Hours: Love Poems to God*, trans. Joanna Macy and Anita Barrows (Riverhead Books, 2005).

CHAPTER 2. CHANGE AFTER LOSS
1. Official Facebook page of His Holiness the seventeenth Gyalwang Karmapa, Ogyen Thinley Dorje, 2 June 2014, www.facebook.com/10737498099/photos/a.73094898099 /10152180146893100/ (accessed 13 December 2021).

CHAPTER 3. WHEN YOU'RE ANGRY
1. Toni Morrison, interview, *The Guardian*, 13 April 2012, www.theguardian.com/books /2012/apr/13/toni-morrison-home-son-love.

CHAPTER 4. WHEN YOU KNOW IT'S COMING
1. Catherynne M. Valente, *The Girl Who Circumnavigated Fairyland in a Ship of Her Own Making* (London: Much-in-Little, 1987).

CHAPTER 5. IT'S NOT FAIR: WHEN A YOUNG PERSON DIES
1. George Saunders, *Lincoln in the Bardo* (New York: Random House, 2017).

CHAPTER 6. SUDDEN DEATH
1. Elizabeth Alexander, *The Light of the World: A Memoir* (Grand Central Publishing, 2015).

CHAPTER 7. IF YOUR FAMILY DISAPPOINTS YOU
1. Charlotte Bronte, *Jane Eyre* (London, Wordsworth Editions, 1997).

Chapter 8. Being Present at the Moment of Death

1. Cornel West, *"Spiritual Blackout, Imperial Meltdown, Prophetic Fightback,"* 29 August 2017, Harvard Divinity School convocation address, https://news-archive.hds.harvard.edu/news/2017/09/08/transcript-cornel-wests-2017-convocation-address.
2. Thich Nhat Hanh, *Essential Writings* (Maryknoll, NY: Orbis Books, 2001), 55.
3. If you're from a troubled family like mine, if you have no family, or if you were abused and treated badly, it might seem like there was no one there for you when you were young and needed someone. But there were—maybe neighbors, grandparents, teachers, nurses, kids at school, or pets. And if you can think of no one at all, remember your own kindness to yourself.

Chapter 9. When You're Too Sad to Move

1. Aisling Bea, interview, *Irish Times*, 2 November 2021, www.irishtimes.com/culture/film/aisling-bea-irish-people-tried-to-connect-my-posh-english-accent-to-some-form-of-oppression-1.4716001.

Chapter 10. Complicated Relationships, Complicated Grief

1. Langston Hughes, "Dear Lovely Death," *Dear Lovely Death* (Amenia, NY: Troutbeck Press, 1931).

Chapter 11. Grieving for Strangers

1. David Mitchell, *Cloud Atlas: A Novel* (New York: Random House, 2008).

Chapter 12. Beloved Pets

1. Jane Goodall, "Jane Goodall Keeps Going, with a Lot of Hope (and a Bit of Whiskey)." *New York Times*, 9 December 2019, www.nytimes.com/2019/09/12/business/jane-goodall-corner-office.html.

Chapter 13. Divorce

1. Jennifer Aniston, "The Unsinkable Jennifer Aniston," *Vanity Fair*, 10 October 2006, www.vanityfair.com/news/2005/09/aniston200509.

Chapter 14. When You're Fired or Laid Off

1. Wangari Maathai, *Unbowed: A Memoir* (New York: Knopf, 2006).

Chapter 15. Loss during a Crisis

1. Erich Fromm, *Man for Himself: An Inquiry into the Psychology of Ethics* (New York: Rinehart, 1947).

Chapter 16. Unspoken Loss

1. Emile Durkheim, *The Elementary Forms of the Religious Life*, translated by Joseph Swain (London: George Allen & Unwin, 1912).

Chapter 17. When It's Time to Say Goodbye

1. David Whyte, *Consolations: The Solace, Nourishment and Underlying Meaning of Everyday Words* (Langley, WA: Many Rivers Press, 2014).

Chapter 18. When People Behave Badly

1. Jack Kornfield, *A Path with Heart: A Guide through the Perils and Promises of Spiritual Life* (New York: Bantam, 1993).

Chapter 19. Don't Be Afraid to Laugh

1. Desmond Tutu, *The Book of Joy: Lasting Happiness in a Changing World* (New York: Avery, 2016).

Chapter 20. Caring for Dying People

1. Naomi Shihab Nye, "Kindness," in *Words under the Words: Selected Poems* (Portland, OR: Eighth Mountain Press, 1994).

Chapter 21. When You're Filled with Guilt and Regret

1. Joseph Goldstein, *Mindfulness: A Practical Guide to Awakening* (Boulder, CO: Sounds True, 2013).

Chapter 22. When You're Lost and Afraid

1. Sharon Salzberg, *Lovingkindness: The Revolutionary Art of Happiness* (Boston: Shambhala, 2004).

Chapter 23. Mourning and Social Media

1. The Buddha, *Dhammapada*, trans. Suttas.com, www.suttas.com/dhammapada-chapter-8-verse-100-115-the-thousands.html.

Chapter 24. Letting Life Unfold—Going Forward

1. Yongey Mingyur Rinpoche and Helen Tworkov, *In Love with the World: A Monk's Journey through the Bardos of Living and Dying* (New York: Random House, 2019).
2. The Buddha, *On Fire*, trans. Bhikkhu Sujato, https://suttacentral.net/sn1.41/en/sujato.

Chapter 25. Honoring Loss

1. Joan Didion, *The Year of Magical Thinking* (New York: Alfred A. Knopf, 2005).

Resources

SAMHSA's National Helpline: 1-800-662-HELP (4357). The Substance Abuse and Mental Health Services Administration (SAMHSA) is an agency within the U.S. Department of Health and Human Services that provides support for those struggling with depression, suicidal ideation, panic attacks, or any other overwhelming emotional struggle. It's confidential, free, and open 24/7, 365 days a year.

Griefnet: https://icwb.com/grief-center. Grief Center is an online internet community of people dealing with grief, death, and major loss. There are support groups and information available free on the site.

Hope for Bereaved: https://hopeforbereaved.com. This website provides information and counseling free of charge to those who have experienced the death of someone close to them. The journey from grief to hope can begin with services provided in groups or one on one.

Option B: https://optionb.org/about. This website is a resource for building resilience in the face of grief, change, or other life challenges. It has videos on coping with hardship, practical advice for talking about loss, recommendations about how to live with health challenges, and more.

Buddhist Death and Dying Information: http://tarahome.org /buddhist-hospice-resources. This webpage has links to Buddhist-related hospice, dying, and teaching resources.

About the Author

Kimberly Brown is a meditation teacher, author, and speaker whose work explores the transformative power and wisdom of love. A Buddhist student for more than fifteen years, she guides individuals to create meaningful relationships through self-compassion, leads groups to develop connection and cooperation through *metta* (loving-kindness) meditation, regularly leads classes and retreats at meditation centers online and in-person, and mentors and trains new teachers.

Raised in the Midwest, Kimberly received a BS from Hunter College in physics and an MA from City College in English. She trained for several years as a psychoanalytic psychotherapist and is a Certified Mindfulness Instructor. She is the author of *Steady, Calm, and Brave: 25 Buddhist Practices for Resilience and Wisdom in a Crisis* and a regular contributor to *Tricycle: The Buddhist Review* and other publications. Kimberly lives in New York City with her husband. You can learn more about her work at www.meditationwithheart.com.